SUCKER PUNCH

ALSO BY SCAACHI KOUL

One Day We'll All Be Dead and None of This Will Matter

SUCKER PUNCH

ESSAYS

SCAACHI KOUL

ST. MARTIN'S PRESS
NEW YORK

First published in the United States by St. Martin's Press, an imprint of
St. Martin's Publishing Group

SUCKER PUNCH. Copyright © 2025 by Scaachi Koul. All rights reserved.
Printed in the United States of America. For information, address
St. Martin's Publishing Group, 120 Broadway, New York, NY 10271.

www.stmartins.com

The Library of Congress Cataloging-in-Publication Data
is available upon request.

ISBN 978-1-250-27050-4 (hardcover)
ISBN 978-1-250-27051-1 (ebook)

Our books may be purchased in bulk for promotional, educational, or
business use. Please contact your local bookseller or the Macmillan Corporate
and Premium Sales Department at 1-800-221-7945, extension 5442, or by
email at MacmillanSpecialMarkets@macmillan.com.

Originally published in Canada by Knopf,
a division of Penguin Random House Canada

First U.S. Edition: 2025

10 9 8 7 6 5 4 3 2 1

For Mom—obviously.

CONTENTS

SAṂSĀRA

CYCLING AIMLESSLY THROUGH EXISTENCE

"I liked being antagonized by him.
He knew exactly what to do."

—KAROLINA WACLAWIAK, *LIFE EVENTS*

PARVATI STANDS
IN FLAMES

⚡

It was boring to talk to God. Any of them, really; at the mandir, my mother would drag me around the main hall to pray to whoever was on deck. We went on Sunday mornings, my sole childhood obligation and my most dreaded one. Forced into stiff salwaars, pushed to play with kids I didn't like, required to eat Indian food for *lunch*, meaning two square meals of my day dedicated to rice and daal and—here's where I would shudder for maximum effect—*bhindi*.

Prayer was a kind of one-way conversation from what I could tell from my mother's performance of religion. The temple was in a remote part of town, a burned-orange building with not even a nearby Mac's to sneak off to for a five-cent Coke-bottle candy. Inside, the hall was awash in a pink carpet, with a red runway to the main deity statues and, of course, the large, clear donation box where you could see how much or how little our congregation cared about the gods. My dad entered our mandir with the authority of someone gracing a party with his presence—he walked gut-first into the room, and sat on the men's side of the carpet, ready for some forgettable chit-chat and maybe a quiet nap in the back of the hall. Of all the issues I had with going to mandir, I was mostly offended that my much-older brother never had to perform any penance.

"Why don't *you* have to go to temple but *I do*?" I asked him when I was six and he was eighteen, when I was several feet shorter than him, my frontal lobe still predominantly soup.

"Just blessed, I guess," he said, pushing me aside and going to his room, then barricading the door to keep me out. And so, my mother would cart me around the mandir to perform the entire family's worth of religious ablutions. It was a lot of pressure.

First we'd visit Ganesh, who was addressed on matters of finances and luck and prosperity. My mother would leave the requisite prasad: almonds, sugar cubes shaped like uncut diamonds, an unpeeled orange, a lit candle. Hands pressed together, she'd mumble to herself something intended just for her and the inexplicably Caucasian elephant she was talking to. Then, she'd leave flower petals at Sita's and Krishna's feet, a couple whose marriage was cemented by Sita's dedication to her husband and to her purity. My mother would pull her chunni—Koshur for a dupatta—over her head, pious in the same form. My eyes would wander while hers were closed. We only lingered for a minute or two per deity, but they were the longest minutes of my life. I was not

permitted to eat the sugar cubes while I waited, like an obe-
dient, bored horse.

But the main event was the display at the front of the
hall, behind the donation box at the end of the red carpet.
A large installation the size of a small playground, on white
steps that were cleaned daily, gleaming under spotlights
and posed in front of draped curtains with gold tinsel sewn
in. There were always fresh flowers and fresh fruit. "Do they
spend all the money on coconuts and grapefruit?" I asked
once, which made my dad laugh, meaning I would not get in
trouble even if my mom pinched my arm like a crab.

The display presented a few deities showered in gold and
fine silks, white skin (why were they always white??), and red
lips. Among the exhibit were two of the most revered Gods
according to my mother's prayers, Shiva and Parvati, parents
to Ganesh, the center of the religious universe my mom was
passively teaching me. Here, at the feet of this altar, my mom
would kneel down—grabbing my arm and yanking me down
too—before stuffing a few bills in the donation box and then
pressing her forehead against the carpet. I pantomimed it
with her and thought about how the soles of my feet and the
crack of my butt were exposed. I was convinced that, surely,
one of the pagdi boys I had a crush on would take this opportunity, my faux worship, to kick my ass. Literally.

What was she saying over there, curled over her knees in
a kind of child's pose, muttering to herself again? I'd lift my
head up for a glimpse at the gods, and always lingered on
Parvati's face. She looked blissed out, like someone who
knew the world's secrets. Her altar was full of crisp apples,

marigolds, waxy cashews, holy water. Parvati would have known what my mom was saying; my mom was talking to her all the time.

Shiva is one of the principal Hindu deities, one part of the trinity including Brahma and Vishnu. Like a lot of the gods portrayed as men in Hinduism, Shiva is cool as all hell. He's benevolent but feared, portrayed bare chested with several arms, one holding a trident, a snake wrapped around his neck, hair in a very trendy half-updo, a look of peace in his third eye but with a promise of brutality if forced. Shiva is known as The Destroyer; he kills demons and protects the universe. I've never understood how modern Christianity became the dominant religion worldwide, when Hinduism offers more gods to choose from, more stories of triumph and deviancy, and a lot of barrel-chested half-men with thick thighs and stoned eyes. What more could you need?

Parvati wanted to marry Shiva; her parents, however, didn't approve. "He had no money, no house," my mom told me. "He put ashes on his forehead. He was wearing—" and here, my father leaped into the conversation as if he had been commanded to by the devil. "A loincloth! Nothing else! Just *kaccha*! Diiiiiisgusting," he said before unhinging his jaw in order to eat an egg, as he does every morning.

"So, he's a loser," I said to my mom, after she outlined the countless ways Shiva didn't make a quality son-in-law despite being a *literal god*.

"None of the gods are LOSERS," my mother snapped at me. "She wanted to get him, and so, she got him."

6

As a show of her devotion, Parvati stands in lengthy meditation for Shiva. In my mom's version, she meditates for fourteen years until she's given a *boon*, meaning a divine blessing from the gods, one that allows her to marry him. But in all my mom's stories, Hindu gods were their most generous selves: they never punished people, they only offered rewards. My mother never talked of a hell, or of getting locked in a reincarnation cycle with no karmic release. Fourteen years sounds like a long time until you delve into more traditional texts, which suggest that Parvati lived in devotional meditation for thousands of years, standing with a foot in five different types of fire. Some versions say she isn't meditating for a boon in order to marry Shiva, but is instead performing this meditation as penance. In one story, Parvati was too playful with Shiva, one of the most powerful forces in the world; when she teased him, closing his eyes in jest, the world stopped still. Hinduism is confusing in this way, depicting the gods as inherently human in their drive for love and marriage and romance, and then celestial in the way they can't sleep at risk of the world collapsing. Maybe that's more apt than I realized—marriage has always felt high stakes, like if you get it wrong, the universe could stop still on its axis.

Parvati's is a story about selfless devotion, proof that time you spend dedicated to someone else—to your *husband*—is time well-spent. It was also a story I didn't pay too much attention to, even though Parvati was everywhere my mom was. In the makeshift temple she built in their guest bedroom, Parvati and Shiva sit together as small statuettes. After my mom showers every morning, she visits their altar there, putting a few carnation petals on their feet or a twoonie nearby as an offering. In fables, my mom told me about all the gods, but I could barely stay awake for her stories about the women. While Vishnu gets to control time and Shiva gets to control space and Ganesh handles gold and Hanuman is a *warrior monkey*, the women are relegated to holding lotus flowers and weeping over their husbands. Why would I need to listen to stories about Parvati at all? I had been raised around women who did nothing but stay devoted to their husbands, even if they didn't necessarily deserve it; my parents are in their early seventies, and still my mother makes my father every shred of food he eats, she sits dutifully by his side while he takes his afternoon naps, she folds every quarter-inch of fabric he wears, loincloth *or* kaccha. I had already seen what it was like to stand in devotional meditation for fourteen years or for a thousand. It looked about the same to me: endless, with limited reward at the end.

Soon, I'd come to my parents with my own plea for marriage. Like Parvati, I promised I knew what I was doing, and like her parents, mine didn't approve. I dug my heels in, my own (loud) form of meditation to prove my devotion. A few weeks before my wedding day, my mother sat with me in a quiet part of the house she raised me in and asked me a question I could never answer: "Are you sure?" I said yes because I wanted to be sure. She gave me the *boon* I asked for, but I couldn't remember why I asked for it in the first place.

✦

Growing up, I spent a lot of time following around my neighbor, Lana, like a sick dog in our suburban cul-de-sac. She was two years older than me, her brother a year younger, and I felt inexperienced and foolish compared with both of them. Everything their family did seemed in diametric opposition to mine, and I envied it all—their whole lives seemed neat, like their life events would be tidily folded at the foot of their beds. They called dinner "supper," a word I had never heard before and assumed it referred to a particularly religious meal eaten at the obscenely early time of 4:45 p.m. They said prayers before their first bite, something I half-heartedly tried to bring back home before my father's vivid sneering told me to stop colonizing my own home. ("Were you *saved*?" he asked me once after I played with Lana for the day. "Did you find *God*?" He said it like it was outrageous that there would only be one God to find.) Lana and her brother put on chaste plays about God in the backyard while I spied on them with my snout pressed against our kitchen window, they read books while drinking unsweetened iced tea (how adult and how disgusting), and did their homework every night before they came outside to play. Lana had an electric toothbrush and always scrubbed for the full two minutes. My bedroom was decorated with photos of Orlando Bloom ripped from the newspaper and centerfold posters from *J-14* magazine, while hers was home to first-place ribbons, little gold statuettes for best bowler or best dance routine. Lana: a true-blue, all-around, absolute sweetie pie. She never yelled, she never fought, she never cried, and she seemed to possess an otherworldly understanding of the universe, even at ten years old. I was never sure whether I had a crush on her or whether I just wanted to consume her, become her, and spit out her silver fillings and blue braces.

I, by contrast, was a bog person. It took me twice as long to learn how to tie my shoes and ride a bike. I was bossy and outrageous and always looking for a way to cheat my way to a win. I had chipped front teeth and scabs on my nose and knees from falling over trying to catch the bus to public school. I talked over movies, a running commentary I hoped Lana would find charming but that clearly got on her nerves—didn't I understand the value of *VeggieTales*? She didn't have an insincere bone in her body, but all my bones were funny bones, which meant I was constantly running afoul of her rules for how to behave. She screamed when I popped the head off one of her Barbies. I thought it would be funny! Her father ran the neck under cold water to shrink it, hoping to force her head back on. The doll lived, but much like me, there was something inherently wrong with her, and Lana didn't want to play with her much after that.

I wanted Lana and her family to like me, but I sensed a kind of condescension I'd experience a few times in my life from white people who believed they meant well. I knew I was a charity case to them but I didn't know why: I had my own middle-class family whose food contained more seasoning than just salt, and I far preferred my parents to Lana's, who seemed cold and distant and always wanted me to call them by their first names, which seemed like asking me to trust a lion by petting the back of its tongue. Maybe Lana knew there was something off about how I was being raised.

I was a little feral, a little toothy. I walked into her house and felt my posture slacken, not because I was at ease, but because I felt like I took up too much space in their stilted air.

I wasn't easy to convert to the world of the well-behaved. Once, Lana's brother scolded me for not finishing a Mr. Freeze. "In our house," he said, "we don't waste food." I waited for it to melt and dribbled the remains into his backpack while he wasn't looking. Still, I wondered if my parents were raising me in some unholy way. Maybe if I followed Lana around more, I could figure out a way to be a little less like myself. She seemed like a good role model. She had such nice dimples; at night, before bed, I'd dig nickels into my baby-fat cheeks and tape them in, hoping to create little divots of my own.

The most abundant differences in how we were being raised, it seemed, were in the communication styles of our families. I never heard Lana's parents yell or curse; mine were yelling so often that silence was more menacing than anything else. This was just how we talked, all of us, all the time. I don't remember Lana being at my house as much as I was at hers; only in adulthood did I consider that maybe her parents didn't want her to inherit our unique form of communiqué.

I wanted Lana to be a confidante but she didn't feel like a safe port. One afternoon, while we played on the monkey bars in the park closest to our homes—well, she played, while I watched like the lifelong hall monitor I have always been, too anxious about cranial injuries to hang aloft from some rickety structure erected by part-time government contractors; what am I, an *idiot*?—I mentioned a fight my mother and I

11

were having. "Paye *thraat*," my mother had barked at me, which roughly translated means, "I hope lightning falls on you." When my brother and I were little, this was a common saying hurled at us alongside a Walmart slipper whenever we did something wrong. In fact, we heard it whenever there was any kind of frustration in the house: My dad screamed it at the VCR for failing to record *60 Minutes* on Sunday, or at the ceiling fan when he realized he'd left it on all day after leaving the house, costing him cents upon cents in electricity costs. My mother swished a half-yard of her robin's-egg blue sari over her shoulder when she said it to me, and I rolled my eyes and barked back, "FINE," as if I could pack my purple-and-pink Polly Pocket briefcase and hurl myself into the sky to find a lightning bolt. I wasn't upset about her saying it because I knew it didn't mean anything—my mother and I were locked in what would end up being two decades of low-grade conflict. All I wanted was a brief respite, a place to complain about my mother and be commiserated with. Isn't this how girls bonded? I didn't have sisters, but I saw something like it on television.

Lana raised an eyebrow the way I had only seen adults do—I didn't know we, as children, had the right to appear so quizzical.

"Wow," she said in a tone that sounded like how her mother often talked to me. "Sounds like *she* wasn't ready to be a mother."

I scratched at the dandruff patch on my crown and waited for the sun to set and the streetlights to come back on, indicating my curfew to go home, so I could unclench my jaw after an afternoon spent trying to meet Lana's high standards. My understanding of my mother's outburst wasn't that she was a bad mother or that she had done anything particularly wrong; she was having a bad day and I was a handful. The story was as routine as me explaining that my mother ironed her sheets before putting them on the bed, or that she did Tae Bo in the basement three times a week, punching the air with Billy Blanks while he counted her down in a shiny blue Lycra one-piece, Jesus, the nineties were so humiliating. My mother didn't mean it, nor did she ever mean any of the unkind things she would say to me throughout my life; she was merely the type of woman who said how she felt when she felt it.

I admired that about my mother, even when I was afraid of her. I was raised on the edge of the working-mother boom, but mine stayed home with me as she had with my brother. *Just* a housewife, people would say. They didn't mean for it to come across as dismissive, but it always did. My mother wasn't *just* anything. She was the most stubborn woman in the world. She seemed to stand sixty feet tall during my childhood. She scared at least a few of my friends, something about the way her brow knit together and made you feel like you were in trouble for breathing. There was no such thing as *just* the most immovable force on Earth.

But this was *just* how we talked. My whole family was loud and bossy and shrill. We got our messages across clearly, maybe brutally, but no one ever missed the point. Every year on my birthday, I would cry over some minor misfortune, and my father would laugh and sing to me: "It's my paaaarty, and I'll cry if I waaaaant to, cry if I waaaaant to." He was mocking me, but he was also giving me permission: *You can always find something to cry about, even today. You're not ruining anyone's time other than your own.* The Kouls are always happy to give someone room to be a bitch.

My mother never apologized for yelling at me—I'm not sure, in her seventy years of life, she's ever apologized, period—but she gave me sliced watermelon as a snack, boondi dahi with dinner, and a slice of chocolate cake for dessert. Is there any apology more universal from an ethnic mother than wordlessly feeding you until you're sick with love? Cantaloupe and sugar prasad were her most reliable forms of communication, the *one more spoonful* was better than any meek apology or perfunctory hug she could've given. If my mother felt bad about whatever she had said, whatever wooden spoon she wielded and then thwacked across my arm, she'd rub my back while I cut into my cake. "You should put your hair back more," she'd say. "I like seeing your face." I could never predict our fights, but I was always happy to forget them on her schedule.

Lana held on to every grudge. I understood the impulse— here I am, thirty years later, writing about a little girl who likely hasn't thought of me beyond the late nineties—but every fight was important to her. She was perpetually exhausted by my aggressive energy. When I fought with my parents in front of her, she bristled and talked about it for days. Her judgment proved to me that she could never really be my friend, and I could never really morph myself into someone she would understand. Over time, I began to think of her as weak. Only the pitiful back down from a fight.

———

I love fighting. I like conflict. It feels natural. And while I rarely won those fights as a child at home, I never appreciated the pretense other families maintained in public. Why pretend like you're not always screaming at each other when that's the truth? I knew Lana's parents fought in that hissy, agitated whisper married adults had seemingly perfected, and I knew her brother was a secret tyrant, but their family was much better at hiding the ugly crags and sharp edges of their dynamic. For what purpose? Who benefits from that kind of tedious deception? What's the point of eating a Mr. Freeze if you hate it? Why finish a meal that will never fill you up?

It's an attitude that, regrettably, has followed me into adulthood. I picked a career that's preternaturally suited to getting into arguments on the internet; somewhere in the 1923 Treaty of Lausanne, probably, it was written into a resolution that any man who disagrees with even half a sentence written in an article by a woman must, by law, send her an email. This joy of fighting extends into the personal, too. Now, grown, living far away from the suburban cul-de-sac that was once my whole world, I'm almost pleased when my mother calls me while I'm in a bad mood. Finally, someone to take it out on, someone who loves me too much to make me face a consequence for my temper tantrum. I *pray* that this woman calls me asking for help on how to set up the same printer they've had for fifteen years, only to discover that they unplugged it at some point and forgot to plug it back in. I sleep the deepest sleep after twenty minutes on FaceTime with her and my father, the two of them trying to aim the iPad camera at the printer, only to angle it so that I can see everything except, incredibly, the printer. ("The screen isn't saying anything because you *need to plug the fucking printer in*.") Daughters seem to choose our mothers for our most loathsome derision; hating her is easy in the same way it's easy to hate ourselves.

But I'll take a fight with a stranger, in a pinch. I like yelling at people in restaurants who are rude to the waiters. I like scolding people for casual littering (why is it still 1982 in New York, people tossing gum wrappers over their shoulders with the casualness of teen movie villains, the sleeves of their white blazers rolled up, everyone inexplicably named Skeeter). I like signing up my old boss for sexually explicit newsletters because he interrupted me once in a meeting. I'm not good at a lot of things—I spent most of high school thinking the word "chaos" was pronounced "cha-choze"—but fighting? I'm incredible at it, and my appetite for it is enormous.

When people meet my parents, fighting as my birthright makes more sense to them. When my parents visited New York a few years ago, a colleague of mine met them, smiled politely, and, as she turned to leave, shook her head and muttered, "Well, that tracks." My parents are incapable of not taking a fight public. My fondest memories are when I was in elementary school, singing a song with my sixth-grade choir, or reciting a poem I wrote about my feelings, and looking out into the gymnasium full of parents and siblings and grandparents, and seeing mine, tightly clenched together, ignoring me entirely and screaming in stage whispers about what kind of paper they should use to line the knife drawer in the kitchen. (The answer, of course, is news-paper, the funnies in particular, because the fading color helped indicate when the paper needed to be changed.) To me, nothing was more comforting than seeing my father's face slowly turn purple, my mother gesticulating with an armful of gold bangles clashing together. I could always find them in a crowd. They were united in the pursuit of raising their respective blood pressures to levels previously unseen in the corporeal form.

People wince when they hear about growing up like this, even people I know who were raised among a similar kind of tension. When I was married, my husband would watch me and my family argue in horror. Despite being the child of divorce and a semi-capable fighter himself, arguments big and small would make him jumpy and tense. Unlike me, he never took any pleasure in watching or joining the argument. When my family gets together at Christmas or Canadian Thanks-giving or at my niece's birthday (her fifteenth birthday is nigh, and in that short time, she has become the most feared person in our family), we just fuck each other up. Remember that time Mom yelled at me about eating too many slices of bacon? Let's dredge that shit up, man! Is it about bacon or actually about how uncomfortable my mother made me about my weight and physical appear-ance? Yes! Let's ruin this nice day! My husband and my brother's wife would hover around us, waving their hands like they were trying to ground a Boeing that's on fire. "Okay, guys, let's all calm down, that's enough." Like Lana, they didn't get it either.

Meanwhile, my family continues to rehash whatever we can, or we look for new, fresh grievances that we can nurse into long-standing grudges. My mother calls me to complain because my brother didn't notice she had a cold the last time he dropped by the house from across town. He emails me later and blames me for not telling him she was sick, as if I should have more insight through my phone calls to our mother and not his ability to fucking see her with both of his eyes, which, judging by how good he is at glaring at *me*, work perfectly fine. I always email him a few days before her birthday and Mother's Day, reminding him to pick up flowers or a card, and he snaps at me that he *knows*, and he doesn't *need* this *reminder* from his *little sister*, despite *asking for it*. We swell, our emotions get huge and bloated, and the house swells with us: my brother is mad at me for being condescending, I'm mad at my dad for being unhelpful, he's mad at my mother for being cold, and she's mad at my brother for being inconsiderate. Our words take up more space than they should, and we drown each other in volume. It's fun! Or, it's not any less fun than the hobbies people picked up during the quarantine. Screaming at your family is a more transferable skill than baking garden focaccias.

The only frustration I had as a child over my aggressive family dynamic was that as the youngest, there was never a chance that I could win the argument; I was always forced to apologize, to change my attitude, to be the loser in an ongoing battle for emotional supremacy. Even as an adult, I still never win a family argument, I am forevermore seven years old, too short to reach the big bowls in the kitchen and too little to watch *Cast Away* without experiencing vivid nightmares about a bedraggled Tom Hanks. But outside of my immediate family, I could have a fair fight. I could be the winner.

The downside of being a grown-up who not only *can* fight, but picks fights to *win*, is that it's wasted on being a grown-up. Everything about being big seems better from a child's perspective: unlimited candy, staying up as late as you want, financial freedom, the ability to touch the genitals of whomever you want and whoever wants you. But then you're an adult, and it looks so much different: stomachaches, exhaustion, a life of perpetual work in the pursuit of the most punishing type of success, and getting a four-day rash from someone who didn't even bother learning where the *c*'s in your name go.

I thought Lana was a fool for not wanting to engage in my terms of enragement. She seemed so cowardly to me, her desire to keep the peace. I knew, for many years, that she didn't like me and didn't want to play with me but did it anyway because she was too conflict averse. She could never say no. That worked fine for me—I had access to her enormous tickle trunk of dress-up clothes and a house that served pork products. But then I grew up, and it seemed less obvious that she was indeed pathetic or foolish. She was being kind, and I saw that as its own weakness. I spent my whole life waiting to fight with someone I love, to be big enough to win. When I got it, it lost any appeal it ever had.

✦

Even now, the word "husband" is still a funny one to me. *Hussssband*. It always made me feel like some kind of Upper West Side mom at lunch who's upset that her Niçoise came with the wrong dressing. Whenever I said "my husband" out loud to anyone, I expected the rest of the sentence to be along the lines of "will be so disappointed to hear about the service here," or, "is really the person you should talk to about this, I don't know anything about our 401(k)," or, "and I are summering upstate, it's such a relief to get out of the city." I really liked saying husband, even if it made me feel like a little girl wearing my mother's heels. At twenty-eight.

Are you married? What story do you tell yourself about your union? Not your wedding day—I don't care what you wore or who came or what your stepsister did to ruin *your big day*—but what story do you tell yourself about how you came together, and what kept you together? I had told our story a thousand times. I wrote essays about him and me and us, and later, a book cataloguing the impossible challenge of getting my aged, tricky, mercurial Indian father to accept my aged, tricky, mercurial white boyfriend. I made money on the story about our fight—I wrote about how my father had stopped speaking to me because I was dating someone he hadn't picked. I turned our fight into profitable art while I wedged my boyfriend further into my family, getting engaged and getting married and making him permanent, like he had always wanted. I bought tickets to Tanzania for our honeymoon on the back of the story about our fight, little gold hoops for my lobes, flowers for my friends, a trip to Italy for my parents for their fortieth anniversary, all from the money made about our fight. On my book tour, he often sat in the first row of libraries and theaters and community centers and smiled, good-naturedly, when I talked about his beefy forearms and stupid face. I let strangers try on my engagement ring, and I reassured audiences that after a year of punishment, my father had begun speaking to me again. My dad grew to like my ex, quite a lot, going so far as to remember his last name; a feat for a man who thinks the high-end department store in Manhattan is called "Bergfordman Bodega-Goodman's."

I was twenty when I met my husband. Now, I'm in my early thirties, the same age he was when we went on our first date. For a long time, the story I told myself about my marriage was one of perseverance, of never giving up the fight. We toughed it out with my irrepressible, pugilistic family who didn't trust him and found our age difference obscene and impure. I had finally, for the first time in my life, won an argument with my family. It had never happened before, and by my late twenties, I felt like I had them figured out. I got to marry someone I loved, in a big, stupid, four-day-long wedding that appeased my parents. But the victory was really mine, and mine alone. My decades of being the too-modern youngest daughter had yielded results: Our family's future generations would remember me like I remembered the cousins before me. Ange was the first to marry a white person. I managed to get one into the family who was white *and* old. I was invincible.

———

Two weeks after our wedding, my husband moved from Toronto to New York to start building the new life I had asked for. Three months after that, I was finally able to join him. (I'm sure there's a joke in here somewhere about the white man in my life getting his visa during a Trump administration in about five minutes while mine took more than a year, but I'm too tired from living through that administration in real time to mine for the punch line. Later, when Trump becomes our cyborg king, I'm sure I'll be able to make sense of those heady early years.) The joyous portion of our first year of marriage was so short-lived that I never even got over the strangeness of saying "husband" with pleasure. Instead, I quickly dove into the strangeness of saying "husband" with rage. *My husband is late* to a friend or *My husband and I got into a big fight* to my therapist or *Don't worry about my husband* when my phone buzzed at the bar and I didn't want to go home yet. We were alone together in a new place we didn't understand, and curled inward in a way I imagine my parents did when they moved from India to Canada. Our immigration stories are vastly different—English was the third language my mother learned, and they were two brown people trying to navigate Alberta, a place that is exactly what it sounds like. But I did grow to understand how they could go from fighting in a restaurant to holding hands while driving home in three minutes flat. Your other was the only person you had. You didn't have friends, you didn't understand the city's infrastructure, you didn't have a relative to run to for comfort. You and your person are alone; eventually, you'll need to get along.

Before I got married, I never understood when people claimed they didn't know why their marriage fell apart. It was incomprehensible to me that you could live with someone every day, that you could have coffee together every morning (his black, as if he was trying to prove something, tea for me instead, because it is socially unpopular to drink eggnog year-round), that you could go to sleep every night with your fingers pressed against the crevice of his shoulder blades, and somehow not be able to articulate when you became strangers. How could you not *know*? Or, how could you not feel it in your sinew that you're losing grip of each other? Wouldn't you just stop the ride and fix it before you fell off? I used to know what kind of mood he was in by the way he turned the doorknob into our apartment; I didn't think it was possible to become so disconnected from the person whose skin felt fused to mine.

My mother reassured me that the first year of marriage was the toughest. But what about the second? The third? Every time I outlined to her a fight we had—sometimes his fault, sometimes mine—she laughed with a mirth I hadn't ever really heard from her. "Couples fight," she said. "Men are stupid. They don't know what they're doing and it makes them panic, like dogs." She'd gesture at my father, asleep in his armchair with his mouth open, as if to say, *This is who you're trying to reason with?*

I should have known I was in trouble when I started to struggle with language, when I couldn't put words to my feelings. Had that ever happened before? No one has ever mistaken me for being verbally inhibited. But I was having a hard time making sense of the hard time we were having. I couldn't find any words that made sense of my constant dread. *Sometimes our fights feel like more than just squabbles, Mom,* I wanted to tell her. *Sometimes it feels like fighting back with him makes it worse. Sometimes it feels like I don't know what I'm fighting for.*

"Papa and I fight every day," she said over the phone. I could hear my dad sitting a few feet away, the whirring of his white-hot laptop whipping into overdrive because he had sixty-eight different tabs of the *Huffington Post* open at the same time. "We fight, and then we get over it. You will, too."

I had indeed spent a lifetime watching my parents hawk-ishly snipe at each other over the big and the mundane. I knew my mother had fought for me, too: while my father and I weren't speaking to each other, she was playing intermediary, trying to warm him up on my behalf. But I didn't worry about my parents being argumentative people because they were well-matched. Papa never said anything to Mom that she didn't have a retort for. He never got in her face. He was never violent or degrading. Their arguments were a series of Kashmiri insults hurled at each other over things that didn't matter: how many plants were too many plants in the kitchen, why someone didn't have their phone turned on while they were at the mall, whether fifty-four degrees Farenheit is an appropriate base temperature for the home. (If my dad is reading this: It's not!!! Take off one of your six sweaters and turn the heat on!) Their bigger, more conse-quential fights—if they had any—were kept away from me entirely. So maybe this was normal. Maybe feeling destabilized was a part of marriage.

Because after all, I got what I wanted, and I got it by fighting. Passively waiting for my family's approval meant it would never come; staying silent and accepting their frosty irritation wasn't an option either. I got what I wanted because I fought. I'm the ur-boxer among the Kouls. Parvati stands in devotion, but I stomped my feet so hard that I cracked the Earth with my heel. I deserved the title, a fact my father would repeat to me in a wide variety of tones as I moved through my relationship. "You got what you wanted!" Papa said in glee after the wedding. "But, you got what you wanted?" Papa said when I told him I didn't think the marriage was working. "You got what you wanted," Papa said in quiet panic when I called crying because I knew I had to move out. On my wedding day, my relatives brought me the same blessings we used to bring Parvati, laid out on a thali: sugar cubes, almonds, a perfectly round orange.

I always get what I want. I'm starting to think that might be the problem.

⚡

I'm at my best when I'm embroiled in a fight. I thrive in conflict, like an oyster that forms a pearl from unwanted intruders. My husband always hated this about me—I listen to reality television when I'm working because it's the only way I can focus, I like to sleep with the windows open so I can hear the neighbors argue, I don't consider an acquaintance a friend until we have a scrap—but it's the only way I know how to be.

Parvati sat at our head table during our wedding reception: instead of flowers, each table's centerpiece was a foot-tall Hindu deity cast in faux marble, their lips and eyelashes painted with precision. On our table was Parvati and her husband, Shiva, with their son, Ganesh, on their laps, and a black lingam with requisite three-striped tripundra. After our reception was dying down, one of my husband's relatives ran around the hall, taking home as many statues as he could. An odd choice for a white guy living alone in a small town, which should give the Feds something interesting to look at when they invariably raid his place for buying too much acetone in Burlington, Ontario.

But I kept Parvati and Shiva from our head table and took them home with me the night of our wedding, as tired as I was. We picked up burgers and fries before going to our hotel, where my *hussssssssband* promptly fell asleep while I ate with one hand and pulled 235 bobby pins out of my head with the other. While he snored, I looked at Parvati and wondered if maybe this wedding, this marriage could be the end of my performances of devotion. I'd shown so much already, in my effort to keep the fight going. Later, when we were so unhappy that I couldn't believe my misery was formed by my own hand—*I married this person? On PURPOSE?*—I thought about Parvati and her outrageous devotion. Parvati always came to mind when we argued, or when we sat across from each other at dinners out, our "time to reconnect." He would read the Bloomberg Terminal and I would scroll through memes on my phone. I thought about Parvati a lot then.

Did part of me like my husband because he guaranteed a fight with someone I love? Probably. We fought our way right down the aisle. But once that was over, and once we were just a couple and my father was finally able to say his name without wincing, there was no fight to be had. I didn't know how to be without an argument. If he and I weren't united against a force, then what were we? Did that make us adversaries? Is my brain that simplistic, that primitive, that if I don't see prey nearby, I'll eat one of my own?

Hadn't Parvati fought the way I once had to? She stood on one leg, in hot coals. How could the texts be accurate enough to capture her devotion, which was rooted in rage as it had always been for me? Her parents didn't want her to marry Shiva, so she proved to them how he was the only man for her. She would torture herself to prove it. That, in turn, would torture everyone else. With my parents too, I had screamed and raged and cried and begged and argued and insisted they respect my wishes. It didn't take millennia, but it did feel like a long time. I won! Then I surveyed my prize, and realized it wasn't much of a victory to begin with.

My ex and I were well-matched in our senses of victimhood. Each of us felt we were standing on one leg, fighting for the other. But I was lonely. I hated New York when we first moved there—every grocery store I went to turned out to be a poorly stocked bodega with a dismissive cat behind bulletproof glass. I wanted to go back home to Toronto and buy an overpriced, watery tomato from Loblaws, the way I was used to. The isolation made me fight more: fighting is a connection, a tether between two people who hate each other because they can't find love. That's the fallacy about hating someone, disagreeing with them, viewing them as your enemy; it's still a form of intimacy. He wasn't good at fighting, even when he tried. He could get some good digs in, but how could he compete with me? He had been adopted into our conflict; I had been molded by it. He'd enter a fight with me, shoulders broad, and he'd leave shrunken. I didn't get it—when my parents fought, they both became big, looming figures. But he just got smaller and smaller and smaller, until I couldn't even feel the mattress sink when he got into bed, hours after I did.

A week before our first wedding anniversary, I felt sure that we wouldn't make it to the second one. We had barely made eye contact for days, and there seemed to be no tenderness left. He couldn't believe how cold I had become, how indifferent I was to how he felt. "Don't you love me?" he asked, and for the first time since I met him, when I was too young to rent a car, too young to drink in Georgia, too young to have to think about death yet, I wasn't sure what the answer was. When I tallied up all the ways he had hurt me, I couldn't believe he was the same person I made all those promises to. When he was angry with me, his green eyes would get greener, making me want to look away. But when he loved me, when he was compassionate, they mellowed into a warm gray. Now, they seemed to be another shade I'd never seen before. Were it a crayon, they'd name the color *remote*.

Here was this lame man, this stranger, this guy I lived

with who had, mere days earlier, ducked when I'd thrown my datebook at his head while he swept up the glass I'd broken right before that. I'd sat on the floor in the hallway of our apartment. My body was hot but the flooring was cool, so I pressed my face down on the ground to bring my temperature down. My eyes had swollen shut from crying and I couldn't pry them open. He put the broom down to join me on the floor.

"My whole face looks like buttholes," I'd cried out. "My eyes and lips are so swollen from crying that I have a face of buttholes. Look at my eyelids! It looks like I need hemorrhoid cream!" I pushed my hair back so he could see all the broken capillaries in my face. He told me that my eyes looked fine, but his credibility was shot. I couldn't trust him; he'd never tell me the truth about my butthole-eyes.

⚡

We were on the brink of separating for good but instead we said: *What the hell, let's go on a quick vacation.* Even in my gloom, I wouldn't cancel a pre-booked train ticket: it was nonrefundable, and I was raised by immigrants who washed out the insides of Ziploc bags. We went north to Hudson, in upstate New York. It's a little village of a few thousand, two main strips full of the most incomprehensibly ugly yet expensive clothing in the state ($295 for a ruffled collar? Not even a shirt, *just* the collar? How do you stay open when your main clientele is exclusively rich clowns?), some perfectly forgettable cuisine, and a lot of Tibetan *namastay-in-bed* novelty T-shirts from nearby Woodstock.

Hudson held my worst days. I slept on the pull-out couch of our Airbnb alone and refused to experience one moment of sobriety throughout the weekend. For our anniversary, he gave me a first-edition signed copy of a book I once adored, and now ignore. It was proof of who he was at his best: thoughtful and attentive, the kind of person who hears you mention a book you love in 2010, and then finds it a decade later at the Argosy Book Store. He printed our wedding photos into a bound book. He looked at me with big, mournful eyes. I gave him a painting that now seems macabre in the daylight of our fissure: A man and a woman, their faces unseen, holding aloft a snake, a flower, and a rotten apple. On the floor is a cracked egg. When your marriage is crumbling, everything feels like a lousy metaphor, and so I quickly grew to hate the painting. I'm still not sure if I'm the woman, the apple, the snake, or the flower. With my luck, I'm the egg.

The night of our actual anniversary, we had dinner at a ghastly but well-reviewed Italian restaurant that the locals all warned us against. The building was clearly intended to be an art gallery, and so we sat at a two-top in the front window on a platform, far from the other diners, like we were on sale, as if a couple could walk by us, point, and say, "Oh honey, I want *that* one." But who would want us? We were a mess. That night was the first in months that he made me laugh. We talked about our wedding—how could this one year have felt so long?—about my dad wiggling on the dance floor, tie off, before holding court with a group of our guests and starting a conversation with, "Well, if you really think about it, there are a few dictators who had a point."

I laughed at my husband's bad jokes, at his feeble attempts to hold my hand, my pitiful attempts to hold his. I laughed when a fire truck parked itself right in front of the window where we were on display, and we became enshrined in flashing red lights for our entire meal. I laughed when the sirens started. I took a photo, as if this might one day be a funny memory we'd want to relive and not the worst weekend of our lives. I laughed when the calamari came out near-frozen and the pasta came out under-salted and too chewy. I drank a martini, then a bottle of wine, then snuck a joint in a back lane as if the police were cruising Hudson for women in their late twenties having mental breakdowns in unlit alleyways.

At the end of the night, I slumped over a bench, the first chill of September filling my lungs, and I cried hot, fat tears. I desperately wished he would touch me but, when he did, I shoved his hands off me. I was terrifically drunk and had spent the weekend crying. I chewed on the end of a cigarette and tried to calm down. He sat next to me in silence—that's all he ever did at that point, too afraid to say a word to me in case it moved the wind in the wrong direction.

When I was finally able to face my husband, his cheeks sallow from our very bad year, I could only choke out one little sentence. "Where," I asked him, his hand warm on the small of my back, "have you *been*?" He smiled at me, relieved that I was still looking for him even when I wanted to cast him out. I don't know what it is, but when your marriage is in trouble, everything feels like a bad metaphor.

I was great at fighting, and my husband was bad at it. And so all weekend, I waited for another fight to come, because I knew I could win. I had been winning them all my life, at whatever cost, for whatever reason. The point of a fight was to win, right? I ignored how this fight felt different, how exhausted I was from our routine of scrapping and then making up until the next argument.

Like Lana, my husband didn't fight the way I did. Arguing with him didn't make me feel safe or heard, in the way that arguing with my family did. In Lana's eyes, being argumentative was a lousy quality in a person, no matter what the argument was about. I began to understand that my husband saw it the same way, by his weak resistance against a personal attack, by the way he'd crumple once the real fighting started. But I thought fighting would give us a framework for a better marriage. I thought it was the first step, at least, in the direction of peace. He never asked me to take his last name but people addressed me by it anyway; the least he could have done, in turn, was learn how to fight so we could communicate in the only language I ever had.

Maybe I didn't want to fight anymore. It wasn't serving me, but how to give up? I had never done that before. No one ever taught me how. The only way to do it would be to question the only identity I've known.

As I limply held my husband's hand in Hudson, I thought

about Parvati, her feet inflamed in the effort to convince other people that her choice was the right one. When we brought her fruit at the temple, did she eat it? Did she peel the oranges herself, or did Shiva do it for her? Did Shiva do anything for her at all, or was she destined for a life of one-way piety? We were leaving her apples and coconuts just so she had something to sustain herself while ultimately prostrating herself for a man.

What was I supposed to do? Sit around and eat fruit?

A CLOSE READ

⚡

"I like that the pandemic happened and all we got was QR codes," Adrian said, spinning a laminated coaster on our table. "Some vaccines, I guess. But mostly? Just QR codes."

I have a small group of friends who all happen to be men, and we informally call ourselves The Hooters Appreciation Society. It started organically enough: For years, I'd text them to meet me for drinks at the Hooters centered between all our offices. I don't *love* a Hooters per se—actually, that's not true. I would step in front of a car for their Daytona Wings and a plate of their curly fries with the cheese sauce, a sure-fire way to shit yourself at 3 a.m., which you deserve, which you have earned. But the best part about taking members of the H.A.S. to Hooters was that I'd come a half-hour later than planned, and arrive to their ashen faces, humiliated by being at a breastaurant without their one token female friend. Who, if not me, would talk to the waitress, so beautiful and buxom that looking at her was like looking directly at the sun? They were almost too afraid to order a glass of room-temperature water. Once I arrived, they'd fill me in with whatever random detail they'd gleaned from the waitress whose double Ds they all worked *very hard* not to stare at. "She says her name is Christmas-themed but she's making us guess," Adrian told me one afternoon as I took my place in the booth next to him. "It's not Noel, Christina, Holly, or Carol. Our next guess is going to be Yule Log."

During the Covid-19 lockdown, I was apart from them all. They lived in Toronto, but I was in New York, struggling through a move I claimed to have wanted. They saw each other periodically, from afar, in a park, behind a mask, but I had to survive off Zoom calls for two years. It was hell, and we were all falling apart in unique ways. Danny grew pustules in some allergic reaction. Sam's divorce was finalized. Adrian grew his hair into some bastardized Tuxedo Mask cosplay, then shaved it all off, making his head look like a brittle little egg, before he broke it off with his live-in girlfriend. (The breakup was bad; we almost called a welfare check on him when he started to toy with the idea of bleaching his entire head. "You're going to look like a fentanyl pop," I told him.) Baby Braga—named thusly for his forever youthful appearance—seemed to start every phone call with a long, shivering groan, exhausted from his various family dramas. We weren't doing well. I'd love to be arrogant enough to think it's because our little group of poop-heads really needed each other, that we needed each other in person, but I know that's not it. Being inside for too long will poison anyone's brain, even the perennially chipper Danny or the overly confident man of average height, Adrian.

But I did feel reassured that it was unlikely that any of my Hoots were doing to anyone what all of my exes were doing to me. Within a few months of the lockdown, almost every man who ever acted like an irrepressible dick to me reached out to remind me about it. Some of them came with half-hearted apologies ("I know things didn't end well . . .") while others, like the boyfriend who once punched me in the stomach in front of a Bank of Montreal in Toronto, merely checked in because he had recently seen me on Netflix and he had a *great* idea for a BMX competition show. Most of them took credit for who I became: "I always knew you were going to be great," one of them said, which *aaaaaalmost* made me forget about how he had a secret family in the suburbs. It was always an insult and yet always hysterical, like getting slapped by a baby. The worst of it was a former TA I had in university, who once cornered me at a dive bar near campus after buying me and my friends drinks and asked me to have an affair with him. I hid in the bathroom and called my friend Barb for advice. *Barb will know what to do*, I thought. *She's mature. She's grown. She's twenty-two.* Barb did not know what to do, and when I left the bathroom, he was lurking outside, and he kissed me. He tasted like sweat and cigarettes, like the feeling you get when milk curdles in your tea. Later, when we returned to our seats at the bar, where Baby Braga smiled placidly at me, *wow, gosh, how cool that our teacher is taking us out for drinks and telling us about the industry*, I just wanted to go home. The teacher's pregnant girlfriend sat across from me at the table, sipping on a non-alcoholic beer, while he crept his hand up my skirt.

In August 2020, that old TA tried to add me on Strava, a jogging app I don't even use. "Accept?" the email asked, as if the site hadn't already trampled on my paper-thin boundaries. *Accept?* Accept *what*? I did that already.

Even my high school boyfriend checked in, years after we had last spoken. I hadn't thought of him since a friend told me he was cracking open my first book at house parties, reading to the crowd passages in which he appeared. That always felt like a real betrayal to me: my old friend, a brown person, too, standing in front of our white classmates like a clown, making fun of me, as if that would give him some cover with them. He got in touch because, for some reason, he had reread the play I wrote about us in high school, a cloying tale about two kids in love who lose touch and are worse for it. I've always loved a heavy-handed allegory; it's a shame I didn't get an editor until I was twenty-two.

"I've had many awakenings over the past decade," he wrote to me during the first autumn of the pandemic. "It took a long time and some brutal honesty to figure out how to lose the ego, soften up, and take responsibility for my emotions by communicating better. I hope we can keep up our friendship this time around, perhaps even become better friends."

For a few weeks, he'd send me micro-apologies as he started to remember—or rather, as I started to remind him—things he did when we were teenagers. Nothing major, just those little grievances that collect for young girls and stay with them through their life: He wanted me to wear cooler clothes. He wished I had bangs (Feist had recently released an album, for which I still have not forgiven her). He made fun of me for the sincerity in my writing.

"That's awful," he said when I repeated my list to him. "Please let me know if you catch me doing that again."

He wasn't all cured, though. When I finally did reread the play, he negged me, saying it was impossible for someone to read as fast as I did.

The resurgence of all these men was surprising because I hadn't heard from any of them during more salient moments in my life or in theirs. A few of them popped up when I started dating my now ex-husband, like they had some radar for when I was dating again, especially someone who didn't think my writing career was "a little hobby." During the height of the #MeToo movement in 2017, I didn't receive one passive check-in, one mealymouthed apology, not even from an editor who held on to my wrist while we talked at an after-party for the National Magazine Awards.

"You have beautiful hands," he said. "You must have beautiful feet."

"Would you get a load of this crown molding?" I said, waving my hands around grandly at the ceiling. "We should talk more about this crown molding."

Anytime I expected something from one of these men— recognition of wrongdoing, maybe a pitiful apology, or learning how to pronounce my fucking name—I got less than nothing. After one of my worst bosses was fired for pinching his employees, he invited us all out for drinks . . . so that we could make him feel better for having lost his job. He once pulled my hair at my desk to get my attention, but now he wanted me to stroke his forty-four-year-old hand and reassure him that he would find work again.

He did, by the way. They all do.

What did these men want, exactly? My high school sweet-heart wanted to apologize to me, I think, but he mostly wanted me to release him from whatever guilt he had developed in the decade since we last saw each other. Some of them, I think, wanted me to confront them so they'd be *forced* to give an apology, and then we'd be settled, all would be square. But the more I think about it, the more likely it seems that they merely forgot. They didn't come with apologies in hand, because it never occurred to them that they might need to. I was a woman they used to know, a girl in a butterfly cardigan and a short skirt in class, ten well-manicured fingers clutching a ticket to her first ever National Magazine Awards, a woman they once kissed on the forehead before saying, "I love you." What's the harm, they thought, in saying hello.

⚡

What else did I do during the pandemic? Hmm, no real hob-bies learned, no new skills acquired. I didn't learn how to keep a sourdough starter *or* a plant alive. I tried to relearn how to knit. I cleaned all my jewelry and then put the pieces back in their boxes. I spent time with myself, and grew to hate her.

Everyone believes they are the narrator of their own stories, but I would've loved to stop hearing from mine. Everything I said or thought or felt was embarrassing and pathetic. I resented the woman living in my head, the way she complained so *ceaselessly* about her relatively blessed, problem-free existence. When I tried to exercise some self-compassion, I fell short because I hated this narrator so much, I didn't want to hear any more of her story.

This is bad for everyday occurrences, but it's significantly, almost memorably worse when your day job is writing. All day you're left with your own thoughts, the stories you tell yourself to stay alive and make a little money. Daily, I was tasked with making sense of my own life and I didn't like the woman I was supposed to understand. I tried rereading my first book during lockdown, as if I could conduct that lightning again. Well, I wasn't reading so much as pawing at the book for hours on end, trying to understand how I got away with taking people's *hard-earned money* for *this*? Most of its pages make me wince, thinking about who I was when I wrote it. A simple little girl, a rube, not a woman but just a series of frayed nerves. The worst of it was "A Good Egg," a near-thirty-page essay about the worst thing that had ever happened to me, which I had squeezed into a narrative that made the worst thing that had ever happened to me palatable.

I don't remember writing "A Good Egg." I don't remember when I first wrote it for an online magazine in my early twenties, and I don't remember bringing it to my book editor three years later with the intention of expanding it. I can't remember coming up with the antagonist's pseudonym—Jeff—but I know why I picked it: it's an intentionally dickless name, one that doesn't scare me.

I barely remembered the events I outlined either: That I loved Jeff deeply, my university buddy who I spent every day with for years, whose alcoholism became too big for me to handle, who slipped away from me as fast as he had arrived. I wrote about Jeff getting rough with me, a clarion call that I'd have to leave our friendship for good. I wrote about Baby Braga, my only remaining friend from that phase of my life, the only person who knew me when I knew Jeff. It's a heart-warming story, allegedly, about my fondness for Braga, and about how I had to cut Jeff out to save myself. Every single word in that essay feels like a stranger wrote it. "Your life's greatest heartbreaks are so often your friends," I wrote. "Dating isn't always built for permanence, but friendship often is." This maxim seems true, but who's this woman who wrote it? I don't know her.

My omissions were never intentional; I wrote that essay unable to fully confront what had happened to me. Instead, I created a story around it that could explain the shape of my devastation but not the depth of it. I tried to sort through my own foggy memory, rereading the essay like it was some code I could crack. I felt the hollowness of my own story. Something was always missing, or was otherwise obfuscated. In my original essay, I wrote that he "rattled my cage." What the fuck does that even mean? Don't I have an editor who can stop me from writing dumb shit like that? [*Ed. note:*

Yes, but do you listen?] There was something about the essay that felt so unwholesome, like biting into citrus still in its peel. Reading it made my mouth taste bitter.

Men lost their minds in the pandemic, but then again, so did I. Only in such isolation would I think to look up Jeff's email address. I was no better than the missed connections trying to reestablish a relationship with me. In the spring, while we were all fighting for toilet paper, I woke up one morning with a sharp pain in my side and looked at my phone for the date. I already knew it was Jeff's birthday. I fell back into an uneasy sleep, dreaming about an alternate reality, one where there was no pandemic, no border closure, no past trauma keeping us apart. If we were still friends, I'd be holding his leg aloft to help him do a keg stand for old times' sake.

I didn't stop to think about what I was doing because I knew it was an inexplicably bad plan. I didn't hover over his old email address in the archives of my inbox, I didn't hesitate to copy and paste it into a new email, I didn't go over what I wrote to him. I remember where I sat in my apartment, what time of day it was, and that I would hide it from my husband.

"30??" I wrote to Jeff. "When did you get so old?"

"Tell me about it," he wrote back two hours later, an email that made me feel like I was being electrocuted when I read it, even though I had started this. I made this happen.

In 2016, when we were twenty-five, I had emailed Jeff to let him know I'd be writing about him and offered him the chance to read it in advance. He turned me down, in addition to my offer to meet for coffee after nearly ten years. "The complexity," he wrote, "lies in the feeling of being 'flattened' when a story you were an active participant in is laid out in ink by someone else. You kind of stare at what feels like a 2D version of yourself with no ability to flesh yourself out into 3D because the narrative has entirely escaped what little grasp you had on it anyway."

I walked around repeating his words in my head for a year. *The feeling of being flattened. The narrative has entirely escaped you. You never had any grasp on it anyway.* I spent so much time ruminating on his assessment of what had happened to us—to *me*—that I clenched my jaw so hard I chipped my tooth. I thought about it at the dentist while she shaved down my enamel. I hated his response all the way down to my bone and sinew. There was no apology, no acknowledgment, not even a nod to the fact that the story contained no elocution about what really happened. I never wrote about how I said no. I never wrote about how he did it anyway. Nowhere did I publish how I timidly put my clothes back on, and asked that he not tell our friends.

I still remember how it felt in that room, the last time I was fully with myself. I remember the sound of the thin plastic mattress in the dorm, how uncomfortable I was, how for weeks after I wanted to peel my skin off and start a new shell. I remember how Jeff's body felt like a swirling black cloud on top of me, this thick vapor that was throttling me. He rattled my cage, sure, but from the inside out, and I could remember him talking to me while he did it, as if it was normal. As if I was even in my body. As if I was there with him. He whispered in my mouth while he raped me and I still remember what he said. I knew he wouldn't; he was so drunk that I could have been anybody.

Jeff said I flattened him in my narrative, which was a strange way to put it, namely because that's how I felt. For a while, I lived like a two-dimensional version of myself, one who looked the same from the front but was barely perceivable from the side. I didn't want him to flatten me twice. This was not a story he lost control of. I was eighteen. I couldn't rewrite the narrative, as much as I tried. All I ever wanted was an apology, and he couldn't even give me that. During the pandemic, with ample time to myself, my memories started coming back, and they all felt lethal. But even still, I sat at my desk and wrote to him on his birthday anyway. I wanted him to look at me, and this was the best I could get.

*

In 2017, when I still lived in Toronto, I went to a screening of a documentary called *A Better Man*, with the intent to write about it. The documentary follows filmmaker Attiya Khan, who interviews her abusive ex-boyfriend, returns to the places where she was abused, and interrogates people who knew what was going on but did nothing. I watched it at a press screening, in a small theater where I was alone for half of the movie—the other reviewer, an older man who seemed disgruntled to be out of his house in the first place, walked out.

The documentary always served as my platonic ideal. Khan interviews her ex, not only confronting him about specific moments of abuse and its impact on her life, but also about what in his history made him so violent to begin with. He answered honestly, with humility and shame. It's a brutal documentary, but she seems to have come out the victor in her life no matter what he did to her. He's alone and terrorized by his own bad behavior; she's married with a child and thriving despite having been abused. I thought about Jeff during the screening, and then almost every day after. I used to hope Jeff would keep quiet about what happened between us; it was so humiliating, this additional proof that I was easy to manipulate. (Once, a few weeks before my wedding, an ex-boyfriend came through town and asked to meet for a drink. I mentioned having been assaulted in the past, and he looked at me stunned. "I never thought you'd let that happen to yourself.") Increasingly, though, I wanted recognition from Jeff. I wanted him to have to look at me and name any one part of what he did.

He didn't keep it to himself, in any case. Stories of our "hookup," presented as vulgar and funny, not to mention consensual, spread within a few months. A classmate chuckled as he told the story back to me, now transformed into an utterly unfamiliar experience, one where I'm laughing along with what Jeff did. "Where is she going?" I heard him ask, as I stormed out of the party after I was told, my ears vibrating with a fresh rush of blood. I went to wait for Jeff at his apartment. I had a key to his place. He had given me a key. I would make myself known.

When I confronted him about it, one of the last times I

looked him in his eyes, I saw nothing more than a vast emptiness. He hung his head and wept silently, his dead face shimmering with tears. He did not say he was sorry. He was already drunk. I'd never see him sober again.

I wrote "A Good Egg" to regain some control over a story I felt like everyone else already knew about me. But how could I correct the record without admitting to what the record was? So I shimmied myself around what happened, and formed a new story that was true, and yet, all wrong. I know I understood the fullness of Jeff's betrayal—Braga and I had talked about it at length. He believed me when most of our friends didn't. I had even told my husband about it within months of us meeting; he walked over from across the table to sit next to me and hold my hand. But hadn't I protected Jeff in my own work, consciously or not? I wanted to save myself, but I carried him on my back to safety. I could have spoken the truth with my chest, but without details that could incriminate him. The whole time, my only concern was how he'd receive the essay, and whether it would have any impact on his life. I didn't want him to get in trouble. I dreaded a confrontation with him, another conversation where he'd calmly question the details of what I knew happened. I didn't want to argue anymore, one of the rare times in my life where I wasn't interested in having a fight. I'd take it easy on him.

Now, I read that essay and know I was a liar.

——

Jeff and I kept talking past his thirtieth birthday and then into mine. I recounted petty squabbles among my newer friends, people he'd never met before. He told me about his parents' recent move, the layoffs at his job, how bored we were during the pandemic's fourth wave. The strangest part of our conversations, though, was how he spent most of them telling me about a girl he had a crush on at work. "She's cool," he told me. "But I don't want to make her uncomfortable, because I'm in management." It was insanity, helping him ensnare this girl into going out with him.

For a year, I didn't tell anyone that I was speaking to Jeff again. I got close to letting it slip a few times, but only with people who were near strangers, halfhearted friends I'd see periodically in crummy Brooklyn bars but who didn't know me well enough to even know I'm Canadian. ("What did you say? *Toque?* What the fuck is that??") Then, as the quarantines lifted, I started telling people I didn't know at all: strangers at airport bars, people standing in line with me at the passport office, women in the bathroom at House of Yes, an acquaintance who I had only met twice before in passing. I don't know how it kept coming up, this teenage sexual assault I was processing at thirty, but it did. I told them about getting back in touch with Jeff, and how unsatisfying it had been, and how I didn't know how to get out of it.

"Why don't you get a new email address," one woman suggested to me, like it was so simple to become a brand-new person, as if I'd never thought of that before. *It's easy! All you have to do is burn your fingerprints off,* Face/Off *your own face, change your name, disappear into oblivion.*

I worked hard to forget where my husband was during this period of our lives. I know he noticed my moodiness and errant weepiness. I know he registered that I would flinch when he touched me on days when Jeff was in contact.

I watched him use my phone to look something up, and felt a flush of panic when a notification from Jeff dropped down from the top of my screen. The message was innocuous, but from a name neither of us had ever uttered at home. "Who's Jeff?" he asked.

"A colleague."

"I've never heard of anyone in your newsroom named Jeff."

"He's in tech."

"Are you friends?"

"Sort of."

If my intention in talking to Jeff again was to get answers, it might've helped if I asked him any questions. Instead of telling him why I was contacting him out of the blue like a surreptitious pen pal, I talked to him about the day-to-day of his life: what he'd had for lunch, how bad his commute was, whether he saw *Dune*. I had real questions. I wanted to know if his memory matched mine, if he was still drinking as much as he used to. I wanted to know if he felt guilty that I gave him a pass on the assault. I wanted to know why he did it, but I was too ashamed, or maybe too scared, to finally cough it out. Whenever I thought through the words I might use, I thought about the color of the condom: blue. Why would they make them blue?

Instead, I turned to my husband for answers. I could tell how much we were going to fight on a given afternoon based on how many, or how few, messages I received from Jeff. Too many and I'd feel put upon, as if my boundaries were being crossed again despite never really setting any with Jeff. Then, I'd recoil when my husband tried to maintain any intimacy with me; I didn't want to be touched, but also, I didn't want to be joked with, joked about, admired, complimented, praised, or even looked at. I didn't want to *be*, quite literally. But if I didn't hear from Jeff for a few days, if he had the *audacity* to ignore my texts about how much I hate the moon, then I'd grow resentful and enraged. "Do you even love me?" I'd ask my husband while he made turkey pot pie. "You never talk to me. You talk to me too much. You're smothering me. You make me feel alone. Don't touch me. Why don't you ever touch me?"

What I really wanted from Jeff was an opportunity to be angry. I wanted him to make a mistake and overstep with me, to push past my boundaries one more time, to force his way into my safe place one last time. I wanted to fight back this time, to scream and flail and eviscerate him. I started to remember, more and more, how frozen I was the night he assaulted me. I wanted to show him what I could *do*. "A Good Egg" was an opportunity to fight back, a moment I made for myself, and then I blew it anyway. I returned back to where I'd started: angry that I never said the truth, with a pen in my hand, determined to write an accurate record for once. I'd be stuck in this ouroboros until I got the story right.

I hoped he'd fall into talking to me about the assault, almost by accident, but Jeff was always careful. He never got too close to me and never asked anything too personal. He never brought up the past. He never said he was sorry. But I never asked for it, I never felt like it was on the table, I didn't think I could take the defeat of another unsatisfying apology. So I demanded it from my husband instead, every minute, every day. I recounted a list of his failures almost weekly, wanting him to say sorry a fourth, fifth, tenth time. I called him all the things I wanted to call Jeff but was, for some reason, too afraid to do so: selfish, cruel, distant, selfish still. Some of them were true, but not all, and certainly not with the intensity that I was recounting. A heat wave settled in New York that summer, and it made me so angry that I almost blamed it on my husband. He was somehow also responsible for my inability to regulate my temperature, as he had been responsible for my galaxy of misery.

Meanwhile, I brought my phone to life and wrote another text to Jeff: "You wouldn't believe the weather here."

⚡

Talking to Jeff felt good until it didn't. It felt conspiratorial and fun, until he said something innocuous that sliced me in half. When he started dating someone new and I asked him if they were "going steady," he scoffed.

"What is this, *Happy Days*?" he said. "Gotta give the juke-box a good thump."

"I'm just trying to be chaste."

"You're known for that," he wrote back. Every few days, he'd say something that felt like a brand-new betrayal. Half of me wanted to give him cover—*Oh, he doesn't know what he's saying*—but how many times in my life could I make excuses for him? At some point, eventually, you have to be aware of how heavy your fists are when you swing them. I'd skulk off, determined to stop contacting him, and fail every time.

Once it seemed like anyone who wanted a vaccination could get one, I traveled to Los Angeles for work, as I once did a few times a year. I'd go and stay in the worst hotel in the city, a wretched, dark little building on a side street in Hollywood, thematically chaotic from the minute you walked in the door until the moment you checked out. The elevator was wallpapered with excerpts from famous movie scripts, there was a copy of the *Pulp Fiction* script in the room, and all the light fixtures were adorned with plastic black-and-white Stormtrooper masks that diffused the light and bathed everything in orange and red. I hated it, but it was familiar: I understood the *specific* way the pillows were too thin, the *exact* way the room service Brussels sprouts tasted like limp, wet shit. Instead of learning about some other place I hated, this place was the devil I knew and I would never be surprised. No one likes getting punched in the stomach, but a sucker punch hurts the body and the ego. I'm tired of being shocked by pain.

My dislike of LA has, regrettably, become a part of my personality, the same way my distaste for positive thinking, most planets, and any kind of health-food sludge have all become a part of who I am. LA makes me feel unsafe. The roads are too wide and the whole city is so pedestrian unfriendly that I await the day I'm hit by a car driven by a Hype House–dwelling influencer who laughs at my cheap shoes. The bars and restaurants are overpriced, filled with semi-famous people who don't deserve a fraction of the respect they squeeze out of waiters and bartenders by screaming, "Do you know who I am?" when they don't get the table they want. Even when it's not hot outside, it's somehow still *too* hot, my neck perpetually slicked in sweat from standing outside an Erewhon after refusing to spend $19.49 on a 750 ml bottle of "purified blue algae water," which I could've expensed, but I was so incensed by the price that I preferred death over giving this grocery store a single red cent.

Halfway through my week in LA, I met with a woman I hoped would result in a fun profile. She was once a famous reality star, a woman plucked out of anonymity like so many women before her who get steamrolled by Bravo or MTV or CBS or Fox. I used to write these profiles a lot, and they all largely followed the same pattern: The women think reality television will offer them some salvation, either through financial independence, or fame, or distance from their families or abusers (often one and the same). But the celebrity and money are short-lived, and they usually end up finding new abusers while on those shows: an on-screen boyfriend who hurls a bed frame in anger, a stranger at a party who accuses them of doing drugs in the bathroom, their face turned into a viral meme before they're even old enough to have a fucking drink. I know how to write these stories because they're all the same, but the readership rarely tires of them and neither do I. There will never be enough time to catalog all the stories of young women who prostrated themselves for entertainment, only to end up with nothing at the end.

Most of the people I speak to for these stories have some kind of self-awareness of who they were and who they became. A few of them—like Courtney Stodden, who went viral for marrying a fifty-one-year-old man at sixteen years old in Vegas—have a profound emotional and intellectual understanding of how they were abused by people near and far, and how much more they deserved. Others don't, but you can still fill in the blanks for them if therapy hasn't done that already. But the woman I was meeting with was different. She arrived an hour late for a ninety-minute interview, disoriented, her blonde hair piled on top of her head. It looked like someone had yanked on her extensions, the beads at her scalp visible at every angle. She looked at me like someone in the depths of a despair they didn't know possible.

I knew the interview was over before she sat down. Earlier that day, she texted me about a recent assault, asking me to take it easy on her. When she eventually did arrive, it was clear she wasn't in the space to be profiled. She told me that her friends left her alone with a man she didn't know, who drugged and raped her when she was unconscious. She told me the whole story, on the record, which even I knew—in my position as a vulturous reporter, out for a good quote and a shitty-as-possible story—was a bad idea. I'm not sure she understood at the time how gruesome her story was. She talked about her assault for a while, upset but seemingly trying to brush it off. "I wouldn't expect you to get it," she said a few minutes in. "You've never been assaulted."

"I have," I told her. "It's awful." She sat up straighter, her eyes childlike.

I don't know why I kept talking to her. I knew it was all unusable, any reporting about this young woman would be a violation of a vulnerable moment. Very little of our interview made sense. Her answers to even the simplest questions would turn into confusing, roundabout stories about how the television network she once worked for abused her, or about how she wanted to become an advocate for young women to stop them from being sex trafficked, or about how she was going home for Christmas to see her family. It was May. I wasn't even convinced she'd remember the conversation once her trauma set in. But she seemed desperate to connect with me in a way I used to do to other women after I had been assaulted. We walked through West Hollywood for a while until we found a stoop and sat there to finish our interview, which had become more like a translation class for me, her answers to my questions a code.

After a little more than an hour, I started to wrap up the interview, very aware that the day was a bust for me professionally, and an incredibly tough day for her personally. She was mere weeks out from the rape. *Her* rape. She was starting to view it, as I have for myself, as an act that she must now possess. It was quickly becoming her burden. "I'm sorry I asked you about your assault," she said. "I don't know anyone else who's gone through this." I told her I didn't mind.

She stood up from the stoop and readjusted her dress, pulling the sleeves down over a bruise I saw on her wrist, thick and green. "Can I ask you one more question?" she asked. "How long did it . . . take you. Like, how long before you felt normal? How long until you were back to who you were before? When did you start to feel better?"

Hearing her question felt like swallowing a wet sock and getting it lodged in your throat. It was a good one to ask, one I've been asking myself for the better part of a decade: When will I no longer be a woman who was raped, and will return to being another woman in the world? When will I feel like who I was before I was eighteen, when I felt like I could walk into any room and talk to anyone I wanted and never feel at risk?

I gazed up at her and tried to smile with my eyes from behind my mask. "It took me a few years to get over it," I lied. "But you never return to who you were before. You just . . . become a new person. You build a new you around what happened."

She nodded dourly. "Okay," she said. "Okay. Nice to meet you." She turned on her heel and walked back to her car while I thought about all the ways I was different now, all the people I could've been without that singular, minutes-long experience.

A few days later while at LAX, I stood in line for an $18 sandwich to tide me over through a five-hour flight offering no in-flight service during the pandemic. Jeff texted me, asking how my week away was going, as he was still in Canada hunting down an available dose of the vaccine. "Productive?" he asked.

"Fine, fine," I wrote. "I was supposed to do one more profile but pretty much immediately she disclosed a rape and didn't seem well, so I don't think I can ethically profile her." Of all the people to tell, I told Jeff. I didn't think of it as a conscious choice, but there was a glee in watching him write and delete replies, the ellipses of his response popping up and disappearing. He was struggling with our shared context, too. What could he say to that? How could he sidestep this one, the closest we'd come to discussing our relationship and how it ended? I put him in an impossible place, and I watched him scramble up the high, unscalable walls of this little prison. I wanted him to starve in there.

"Shit," he said. "That's a whole thing." I turned my phone on airplane mode and brooded for the full flight. I've been working through this for my entire adult life. Not a day has gone by without me trying to figure out the right words to say about it, the right essays to write about it, the right feelings to comfort myself with. I wasn't sure how much Jeff thought about it, but I know I thought about it more. And with one text shot into the sky, he summed it up in a way I never thought to. He's right; it's a whole thing.

I never wrote the profile, but I also never forgot the interview, never forgot how she looked at me and how familiar that facial expression was, and how I immediately knew it was one I'd made myself. Shell shock. I couldn't believe that after all this time and all this work I had done on my own, he'd won one more fucking time.

✦

While I tried to decide what to do with Jeff, I went through yet another period where I was the main character on my little corner of Twitter. After writing a profile of a YouTuber, my mentions and DMs were throttled for days with people demanding I be fired (it really would take much, much more), demanding the article be taken down (and lose all this sweet traffic?), and generally calling me a shitty journalist and a bad writer. I can handle most of that, but the part that did pierce me were the people who believed I was letting a rape apologist off the hook.

The YouTuber was in the midst of what would end up being a series of intractable internet snares. This time, viewers were outraged that the YouTuber in question had stayed friends with another influencer accused of rape. In the time I spent reporting on the story, I never got any clarity on what happened during the alleged assault, or whether the subject of my profile knew about it in the first place. That didn't matter to the bulk of our readers, who called me a rape apologist, saying my story was tantamount to abuse.

Most of the people tweeting at me were very young, and almost all were women, which suggested to me they had their own stories of their own assaults. People who didn't believe them. Friends who picked the wrong side. I had, inadvertently, stepped into a conflict that sounded so much like the one I had already lived through. These women wanted me to score-settle, to *proclaim* how unfair it is not only to be assaulted, but to then have to fight to keep your life the way it was, the way you liked it. You have to fight to keep your friends on your side, and they wanted me to play referee.

I couldn't tell all these people that their anger was misdirected. I started having dreams of standing on a soapbox in front of all their avatars and their Twitter bios. "Guys. Guys! Come on. I'm on your side! I just have to take into account the antiquated but firm rules around defamation! I'm a 'survivor' too, okay?" It's not like this would've worked, but it also wouldn't have been fair: everyone is entitled to their own interpretation of writing, to how their grief might intertwine with that writing. My own position as someone who had survived an assault didn't take away from their upset, nor did it mean I was a perfect interlocutor of that experience. These girls were owed their rage.

Then again: maybe I deserved it. These readers were holding on to their fury, and I was still busy trying to forget mine. I didn't want to be mad anymore, and I didn't want to fight. I had done so much of it, and seen how limited the results were. Unusual for me, I wanted to be at peace again, even if it meant patching things up with Jeff. I had started to believe he deserved it, this redemption without doing any of the work. I wanted the man who took so much from me to take one more thing—my dignity—and mail it back to me with a kiss.

Like always, when anything happened that made me feel as though I was being run over, I went to Jeff with it. "I am . . . getting the shit kicked out of me on Twitter," I wrote to him.

"Go look up my first name. I dare you." He had already read my piece, which made me both blush and tense up—was he secretly following me on Twitter this whole time? Was he watching me even when I was working so hard to forget what it felt like to be looked at by him? Did he ever actually make eye contact with me, or was he always looking at the meat of my bottom lip?

"Honestly, this is scrambling my brain," I told him. "I feel normal and then periodically, I'll stop what I'm doing and be like, *Wait, am I the worst person in the world*?"

"No, you're not," he said. It was the most succor I felt that whole week, before I steadily started to feel sick. I had sought solace in the man who made the idea of me being "a rape apologist" so absurd in the first place.

⚡

A whole year passed and Jeff turned thirty-one. It felt perverse to have spent this entire year in contact with him with no plan, no idea what I was even going to do about him. For a year, he felt like a problem to be solved, but solving it meant we would be over. I would, again, have to let him go. I'd again have to worry about what he might say about me to other people. I would, again, have to explain to my friends why I was so sad.

My husband and I went to Miami for a long weekend to celebrate his birthday. By that point, our marriage felt like splintered glass, where even the finest touch could crack the whole thing and send it shattering to the floor. I still hadn't told him I was speaking to Jeff again; why bother, I figured, to inflame him all over again with details of my assault. But during dinner at a too-quiet restaurant, we went over the list of men in the media industry who had harassed me throughout my relatively short career, a list that included countless mutual acquaintances we had. It wasn't our typical dinner conversation, but I wanted to talk about something that made me feel like we were on the same side. Our relationship was already hanging on by the most tenuous thread we had left; maybe if we talked about all the people who tried to ruin us, we could find each other again.

"Remember that guy who tried to get you to break up with me?" he asked.

"Remember the guy who invited me over to his house because he was going to 'order me a cab' but instead he wanted to watch *Atonement* and then tried to kiss me even though I had the flu?" I asked.

"Remember the guy from *The Globe and Mail* who kept flirting with you even after I told him you and I were dating?" he asked.

"Remember the guy who kept interviewing me for a job that didn't exist and the interviews were always at night and always at a bar and he was always buying my drinks?" I asked.

"Remember that parking lot fistfight I almost got into?" he asked. That one I remembered well; my husband and Jeff had run into each other at a party, without me, almost ending in blows. Even secondhand, the story felt humiliating to me. I was able to keep my cool with Jeff; why couldn't he?

I demurred, as I always do when Jeff comes up in conversation, but this was worse, because my husband didn't know we were back in touch, and didn't know that I waited by the phone for those little *pings* to arrive. "Well, maybe he's different," I said. "That was a long time ago."

At our little dinner, my leg shaking furiously under the table, I finally told my husband about how Jeff and I had reconnected. His barely concealed rage was well beyond what I expected. Waiters looked at us as I cowered to my partner, who was keeping his voice at a loaded whisper which scared me more than any screaming match ever could. "Are you stupid?" he asked me, and it did occur to me that, well, yes, I think I might be. It was my fault, I know—who brings something like that up on a *birthday*?—but I couldn't help it. I was hoping my husband would moor me, would pull me back in to his safe harbor. He didn't, nor did he seem to want to. All the stories I had told myself about other people were falling apart: Jeff was not pure villain and my husband was not pure hero. I was hoping that a man, any man, would give me clearly defined roles. If he's the good guy, I can run into his arms and be safe. If he's the bad guy, I know where to run from. Neither of them were turning out to be who I thought they were.

My husband looked at me with disgust. Indeed, I never thought about how my husband would feel knowing his wife was texting another man. I was foolish in that way, and selfish: I wanted to own my wounds. He took them over and made them his. My lies hurt him the most.

"Why do you think he'd be different?" he asked me, throwing his napkin on the table. "When your book came out, did he apologize? Did he realize he did anything wrong? Did he ever acknowledge that he did anything wrong?" My ex was right about a few things: none of the men in my life ever apologized, not even him. What was I hoping for?

He stormed off and left me to go back to our hotel alone. My phone pinged throughout the night with texts, but I knew it wasn't my husband coming to look for me.

⚡

Jeff and I stopped speaking after my husband's cursed birthday in Miami. It wasn't so much that my husband's fury made me rethink our conversations, but rather it proved I was looking for a fight when in fact I had no taste for one. I came to Jeff geared up for a confrontation, one I figured I would eventually prompt. Instead, I had those fights with my husband, and they were wholly unsatisfying ones, too. My confession to my husband changed the texture of my conversation with Jeff. I had been reaching around in the dark looking for meaning; now, the lights were on, and I saw that I had been grasping at air.

Jeff and I ran out of things to discuss—you can only have small talk with the person who fundamentally reshaped your relationship with men and your own body for so long. We lost touch, as they say, a troubling turn of phrase for someone who had seemingly been touching me from afar for more than fifteen years. Without a fight, we had nothing in common anymore.

For years, I had struggled to see Jeff clearly. I mean this literally: I couldn't imagine his face, and seeing photos of him never quite captured how I had felt looking into his eyes. I could only visualize his hulking frame when it stood over mine. I could only remember how tall he always felt to me, how barrel-chested, how angry he once got when he was drunk and wanted to rip a stop sign off a street corner. I could remember him shoving me that one time in his apartment, against the stove, an imprint of the door's handle in my lower back. He became bigger and scarier and more daunting. I lost perspective on him entirely. I couldn't remember his voice. In his absence, I could only think about what he said to me while he was assaulting me, while I was saying no. We were in the middle of a fight in a dorm room about his dishonesty; I remember him putting on a blue condom while he repeated, "I don't lie; I omit." He always emphasized his *t*'s more than I liked.

Jeff died when we were thirty-three. Back when we were kids—Braga, Jeff, and I—we'd talk about which one of us would die first, and we always knew it was Jeff. Together, we'd joke that it would be from some freakish accident because of his tricky wiring; Jeff liked to fight, liked to run, liked to steal. He was impish and immature and always tripping on his own bad decisions. We laughed about it, but privately, Braga and I knew it would be more dire and more inevitable. I didn't know he was in the hospital until he was already gone.

In death, Jeff's life opened up to me. I learned more about him than he had shared with me when we were speaking. He got a new job. He lived in a new apartment. He switched brands of cigarettes. He started drinking a kind of beer I had never heard of before. In photos of him close to his death, he looks wan and weak; I can't imagine being afraid of this person. His eyes didn't focus in photos; they darted in opposite directions, detached from his smile. The girl he had a crush on at work, who he wrote emails to me about, ended up becoming his wife. His widow. The same words of ownership I used over being sexually assaulted ("my" rape) are the ones he would use for this person who he seemed to love a great deal. *Mine mine mine*, now *hers hers hers*. I felt reassured that he was never alone, even in death, and then furious that I cared about whether he was alone in death in the first place.

I had told my own story, falsely, in my twenties because I wanted to protect Jeff while also making sense of what he did to me. "Rape" is such a big word. I don't even like reading it. It took me over a decade to call it what it was, and as soon as I was able to, he died. "I felt exposed," I wrote a decade ago, "rattled, his body hanging over me like a threat I always knew was there. My wrists were left with red marks from his fingers. It was the least fun we had ever had together." I always knew what Jeff had done to me, but still I split him into two people: one, the man who raped me at a party when I was barely an adult, and two, the weakling who needed me to help him reform. Now, he has once again taken the narrative with him. When he was alive, I was determined to protect him even if I had a primal need to speak out loud what had happened to me. Now I'm free, and I'm ready, but instead of feeling relief, I feel guilty about speaking ill of the dead.

Online obituaries from his friends mentioned how troubled he could be, how relieved everyone was that he could now find "peace," but none of them directly said the truths we knew about him, the ones that often contradicted themselves. I wanted to know if Jeff was rehabilitated after he assaulted me. I was worried he had done it again, or had some predilection for it. I don't know if he did or didn't, but it seemed like he had changed since we knew each other. He held a job for as long as we weren't friends. He met someone lovely. Maybe he was everything I was hoping he could be. Schrödinger's cat can turn out to be a nice surprise; it doesn't have to be a looming threat. In his death, I can choose to believe that he tried harder. I'm left with wishes that will go nowhere: I wish he hadn't raped me, but he did. I wish I didn't have to rehash it again for my own survival, but I do. I wish he hadn't died, but I have no say in the matter. I didn't attend any of the services. I didn't send flowers. Instead, I thought about sitting next to him in class, sliding the sleeve off his coffee, and drawing a watch on it for him. He wore it all day. I loved him so much.

Now, I see Jeff clearly. For most of my life, he has lived in my heart with either extreme affection or extreme prejudice. He mattered to me, all the time, even when he wasn't around. It felt like, for years, he made every decision for me. Falling in love with someone older, protective, and angry was a response to him assaulting me. Running away from Toronto was another attempt to avoid reckoning with the kind of girl who would "let something like this happen" to herself. And, ironically, kick-starting some gupshup with Jeff during lockdown was my own way of avoiding the more urgent fight happening inside my marriage.

Some of "A Good Egg" was true, but I turned a story about rape into one about friendship, a safer place to hide. My fight, here, dies with Jeff. I can't restart this conversation with him again, I have no further opportunities to ask him why he did what he did to me. I have nothing else to fight for, or about. I know what happened; his refusal to own his deed won't outlive him. I will.

I used to write cleaner essays, stories where everything ended with a bow. All those men reached out to me in the pandemic, but the only person I wanted was the one who'd never come calling: I went after him myself. He offered me nothing, so I set out to try to take it back. I wonder what those men wanted from me. What were they hoping to take back?

I wish that they'd ask. I want to say no. I want to refuse them further gifts. I want to deny them any more pieces of me.

I see Jeff everywhere now. I bump into six-feet-tall men on the street and think it's him. I see babies on the subway with his cloudy eyes and upturned brows. I hear him in pubs and sports bars, filing in and out of Barclays Center during basketball season. When the wind knocks me over, that feels like Jeff, teasing me on the way to class. He's shrunken back to normal size, just a boy I knew, not a man worth fearing. I see versions of him everywhere, these men who can't help themselves, and I feel myself wanting to rush after them, tie their shoes for them, tell nicer stories about them to keep the peace. So much of me is still determined to believe a man's fable about how he has rehabilitated himself. I'll do it at my own cost. I'll edit my own story down so that the reader laughs instead of winces. I'll find empathy for the villain, and turn him into an antihero. I used to feel safer in stories where men hurt me only when I deserved it.

But can't I own my own stories thanks to the simple fact that they happened to me? They're mine, aren't they? The story is the only thing I get to take with me, wherever I go. The lie of it was never sustainable because it was always in service of a man who didn't deserve my restraint.

Jeff never apologized, so I've done it for him. We never got to say goodbye, so I have to do it on my own. The clearer I see him, the clearer I see myself. I've always felt guilty about writing about Jeff, even now as I write this. But in the same email Jeff sent me complaining about being "flattened," he signed off with a kindness that I didn't commit to memory as much as I had the cruelties. "You're gonna write what you're gonna write, and that's none of my damn business, nor should it be," he wrote. "There's no opposition coming. Weird as it may sound in this context, I'm proud of you." I see him, and I see myself.

KARMA

THE CONSEQUENCES
OF OUR ACTIONS

"Of course I'm writing this later,
much much later, and it worries me
that I've done what I usually do—hidden
the anger, covered the pain, pretended
it wasn't there for the sake of the story."

—NORA EPHRON, *HEARTBURN*

CHOCOLATE, LIME JUICE, ICE CREAM

⚡

Here are some things I would rather do in public than write about my body and, specifically, my struggle for self-esteem: punch my cat in the face, eat a leech, have sex with an impolite wolf, allow someone to watch me try to pluck an ingrown hair from the most tender part of my groin while hunched over myself and squeezing a little pustule until it pops and mixes with blood and turns pink and I groan, satisfied, "Oh, *gross*," while pulling out a follicle the length of a cucumber. In fact, I would far rather present to you all naked, in this exact body, in public, than actually *talk* about my body. I'd prefer to show you so I can avoid acknowledging this vessel, which I've worked so hard to hide.

All indelible memories are rooted in trauma, like trees grown in a dumpster, all crooked and ugly and covered in leaves made of used diapers and stretched-out Fashion Nova tops. Naturally, some of my most vivid memories are those where I discovered in what unique and particular ways my body was *wrong*. By the time I was nine, I was well aware that I was too hairy, too brown, and too big. It's unimportant whether any of those factors were true; they were true to me, and true to my white, hairless, skinny classmates and friends.

Tiny and I were friends through our moms, both Indians who knew each other in the community. I never knew if Tiny and I were all that compatible as friends, or if we knew that our moms would let us hang out because we were shaded the same way. Sleepovers were an easy thing to sell to our Indian moms, who seemed reassured that the other would rest in a safe place. I spent weekend after weekend at Tiny's. Her place had a big front courtyard where we played basketball poorly, a cuckoo clock that was disruptive and ugly—something that fun would never exist in my parents' home—and a desktop computer in a dark room where we could google pornography and flirt on MSN Messenger with Tiny's non-blood-related cousins. A rite of passage for South Asian girls everywhere.

Tiny and I bonded over our bodies. Before we were old enough to know the words "sexual exploration," we looked at each other's vaginas and compared notes. Ours were similar in shape and color, which felt like valuable data points. We spent one sleepover balancing Barbie teacups on our completely nonexistent breasts. When we got older, we talked about how much we resented the ever-darkening hairs on our arms.

But unlike me, Tiny was skinny. She operated with a kind of ease among other girls our age that I always credited to her weight, though we never discussed it, of course. I felt my body was growing too fast and too wide, stretch marks lining my legs and gut, but bringing it up would mean recognizing it as true, which I couldn't bear to do. I admired Tiny's raw-boned legs and arms, her square, flat torso, her collarbone protruding when she laughed. She looked like a little girl, age-appropriate in her smallness, and I felt like I looked like an old woman, with a cafeteria-lady ass. Maybe that's why boys were so unkind to me; prepubescent, I gave off the energy of a divorced woman in her late forties. (My destiny.)

Sometimes, Tiny would invite one of her white friends over. We went to different schools, and the white girls I was friends with were clumsy, dorky, sweet, and friendly. Her white friends were tall and lean, popular and blonde. Their mothers had *jobs*, and they took the *city bus* home from school *on their own*. Mine wouldn't let me cross the street without a chaperone. They were the meanest girls I had ever met in my life and their hair smelled like strawberries. I'd walk behind them, sniffing, my body lifting in the air like I'm Yogi Bear and they're a pic-a-nic basket made just for me.

One Saturday after yet another cosmically humiliating swim class, my mom dropped me off at Tiny's house while she was hanging out with one of those mean, beautiful girls. We walked around her sleepy neighborhood, lazed in the sun in the backyard, fussed around with Barbies we felt too old to be playing with. I was still in the fifth grade, but Tiny and her friend were two full years older than me. They were grown. They had seen the world.

I never really knew how to bond with girls—I still don't, which means I generally offer to buy a round and then ask everyone about their skincare routine—but making fun of our moms was a win. I knew how to imitate my immigrant mother, to make fun of her lilting accent and her penchant for dropping the definite articles in her sentences. I could put a hand on my hip and swivel myself in an invisible sari to the pleasure of little racists all over suburban Calgary. (My mother never wore saris to lounge around at home; I was only ever appealing to the lowest common denominator.) At the time, I wasn't bothered by dehumanizing myself *or* my mom, who surely would've popped me clean in my front teeth had she ever seen me mimic her as if she was an Indian Mrs. Roper. But I was worried about being seen too closely by girls like these, and making a joke of the person who loved me the most in the world was good deflection.

"Oh my god, my mom's crazy too," Tiny's friend told me. Tiny had gone inside to sneak us a few Cokes, drinks that were restricted from us unless at dinner parties filled with drunk Indians who weren't paying attention. Left alone with Tiny's friend, I felt wired by the blush of her attention, her full eye contact, which I received because there wasn't anyone else around. "You know the old saying that you get one roll on your stomach for every kid you have? Well, my mom has had *three* kids, and she only has *one* roll. But she's always talking about being fat! Isn't that so crazy?" She motioned to her midsection when she talked about rolls, drawing big semicircles with her hands over her stomach.

I had, simply put, no fucking idea what she was talking about. I was eleven. What "old saying" would I have known about body fat at eleven? It was the year I got my period, the year I started touching myself over my underwear, and the year I got a computer. I had other things to worry about than old wives' tales about how many stomach rolls an adult woman should or shouldn't have based on how many kids she poops out. (Incidentally, at eleven, I still thought babies came out anally.)

But the comment was enduring: here I am twenty years later, still thinking about it. Her words climbed up and down the walls of my head for the rest of the day at Tiny's house, like a spider with a sac full of eggs that would soon crack and infest. When her mom made us cucumber sandwiches, I considered the Amul butter she used. When we went to Tiny's room to dress ourselves up in her clothes and put bindis on her white friend (we were experts, after all), I suddenly didn't want to take my shirt off in front of a girl I had known since I was three. And later, when I came home and took a bath, I inspected my midsection in the reflection of the faucet. There, distorted in the metal, were my budding breasts and three perfectly identical tummy rolls. I ran my hand up and down the terrain of my body. I was craggy and bouldered, like a street lousy with speed bumps.

I had *three* rolls, and I hadn't even had *one* kid. Tiny's friend's mom had *one* roll, and without ever meeting her, I knew she was one of those beautiful, young white moms, the type who wore a thick ivory wristwatch that looked like money, who had her hair brushed straight into a severe, honey-colored bob that she got blown out twice a week downtown. How had I let my body get this out of hand?

Our mothers are the soil of our trauma, and they grow us tall and formidable and a little broken at our cores. If it hadn't been Tiny's friend seeding my body complex that day, it would have been my own mom. While I was inspecting the way my stomach creased when I sat down, my mom was in the kitchen portioning out bland chicken breasts and a quarter cup of rice for her dinner, trimming asparagus that would be blanched to taste like piss. I thought that's how all mothers ate. I figured that one day, I'd have to eat like that, too. That becoming a woman meant restricting yourself from one of life's greatest pleasures: a calorie consumed without thought, without anxiety, and without self-critique.

By the time I was in high school, I was throwing up daily. I punctuated the ritual by looking at my stomach when I sat down. No matter what I did, I still had my three rolls despite never having any children. I was a tree growing in the darkest organic shit known to man: a woman's body-panic, passed down, metastasized and sown.

⚡

In *More Than a Body*, authors (and twins) Lexie and Lindsay Kite ask their reader to think back on a time when they weren't self-conscious about their body. "Take a few moments to remember a specific experience from your childhood when you were free from self-consciousness about how you looked or how others perceived you," the book says. "You are more than a body, and you knew that once."

Such a moment doesn't exist in my conscious memory—I know it must've happened, but when? Even at five, I remember pulling a corduroy dress over my shoulders, and thinking that I was surely the only person in the world who had that pocket of fat hang between my not-there-yet breasts and my arms, that little flap that looks like a vagina. Was I supposed to tuck it in? I asked my mother to put a T-shirt on under it, a protective layer, as if it could hide my body from everyone in kindergarten. She obliged; she thought I was being modest.

Even during the apocalypse, I was calorie counting. I was still following The Rules, a set of requirements around my eating that I've had since I was twelve. The Rules have changed over the course of my life, but there are always Rules. In the early days of the pandemic—already anxious enough about my parents being trapped in India, my inability to return home, the government building a hospital in Central Park *just in case*—I was still counting my 1,200 daily calories, refusing myself bread and rice, sneaking a cookie and then thinking about it for the rest of the day. This was normal, a typical pattern for me, to eat and self-flagellate, but now layered with the added stress of possibly dying from an unknowable virus. I couldn't stop myself: I'd wander out of my house after days of being stuck inside, buy a coffee and a croissant with the anxiety of someone being hunted for sport, and then weigh myself after I devoured its crumbs, surprised that I could gain a few pounds during the day. I felt like I would surely die before the end of the year, along with everyone else I had ever known, our lungs collapsing from Covid-19, but first, it was very important that I feel bad about carbohydrates.

I knew it was dumb! I did it anyway. In my late twenties, I had fantasies about how my eating disorder would eventually serve me. Maybe I'd get run down with some illness that sapped my appetite and I'd lose weight that way. Maybe I'd become bedridden and incapable of consuming more than clear broths and blanched carrots. Or, *ooooh*, maybe I'd get a tapeworm, and the tapeworm would eat all my food, and then I would become thin *and* have a gross but fascinating story to tell at dinner parties (where I would never eat much, of course) for the rest of my life.

While we all huddled indoors for what ended up being nearly two very surreal years, I thought about how I could emerge from my personal pandemic a little bit better, a little bit more beautiful, a little bit more desirable. Maybe if I worked out really hard and made healthy lunches and cut down on my after-work drinking, I'd emerge skinnier than I'd ever been in my life. This was my time to pupate, if only I could stop the stress of the pandemic from making the rest of my body rebel against me. My eyes started chronically twitching, my muscles ached every day, my teeth chipped, my nails peeled, and my hair fell out. But was I getting thinner? That's all that mattered. Were my skirts looser? Was I shrinking? I hadn't made myself purge since I was in my early twenties, but now I had all the time in the world to inspect myself, to criticize every morsel I let enter my body, to work out a way to make sure it would be a demon exorcised before the next mealtime came around.

I have always been like this, and it's humiliating. And then, as I cut into these layers of mortification, I'm humiliated because feeling like this is so *mundane*. I have yet to meet another woman who doesn't eventually admit to having the same insecurities, the same anxieties about their size and shape, how much space they take up in a room, how they feel if a chair creaks under them. I've heard it from skinny women and fat women, women who exercise fiercely, women who count calories obsessively. I've heard it from women who do none of that, who try to disengage from the rituals of self-loathing; they, too, know that escape isn't so easy. I'm mad at myself for being mad at myself, mostly because it's such a jejune affliction to have. We all feel the same way, all the time, no end in sight! Couldn't I instead have one of the more interesting entries of the *DSM-5*? A compulsion to eat dishwasher pods like the women of *My Strange Addiction*? Maybe a brand-new psychological dysfunction that they could name after me: Koul Disorder, the unexplained impulse to flip off any camera taking a picture of you at any time, exacerbated by baby showers.

Before my wedding, I wrote a short essay about how much I resented having to think about my body in a dress, how much I hated feeling like I *should* lose weight even when I really did want to. After it was published, Braga timidly mentioned that he did, indeed, notice that I always had a tough time with food. After more than a decade knowing each other, I had never talked to him about it once.

"I mean," he said, "I knew you were always on some kind of all-quinoa diet or whatever." I still have not recovered from such an assessment of my eating disorder. *All-quinoa diet???* I can't believe he knew I was insane this whole time and he didn't even say anything!

So what do you do to stave these feelings off? What are the things you do to make yourself feel like you look smaller than you are? Not what you do to make yourself thin—most of us know what those things are. We avoid carbs and dairy. We never eat dessert. We don't drink soda pop with sugar in it and our only cocktails are Tito's on ice. But what are the little things you do in order to merely appear thinner, perhaps while you're doing something that doesn't necessarily move you toward the pursuit of thinness?

I pull on my shirt when I sit down, tug the fabric away from my midsection. I press my tongue against the roof of my mouth so that my chin appears more defined. I like shirts with sleeves. My shoulders sometimes feel inappropriate in meetings and at work; my body is inherently too sexual because there's plenty of it. My chest: there is just so much of my chest, such a vast expanse of skin. It is a legal mandate that any pants I wear have some sort of elastic to them. I'm never entirely sure who any of this is for. No one is paying attention other than me. Or at least, I'm paying the most attention.

There's something despicable about the conspiratorial way women talk to each other about food. "Should we get dessert?" we ask each other, looking coy, as if we're asking if we should both do heroin in the streets. "Oh, let's be bad!" we might say when ordering queso. "We've earned it!" is another one, as if food is something you're allowed to have only if you put in the requisite work beforehand. "I'll get it but only if you share it with me," is a fun one. When on assignment with another reporter, whose slender body was partially the result of her not eating for days on end (so she told me, casually, as if food was optional the way manicures are), I suggested we order a pizza to our hotel to celebrate locking down a new source. "I love this version of you," she said. "You're so . . . indulgent!" I didn't eat pizza for a year after that. It wasn't her fault. She didn't know what she was saying. Or rather, she did, as we all do: she rose from the same shit-soil that I did, too.

⚡

It's rote for a woman to blame her issues with food on her mother, but cliches exist for a reason. One Saturday, when I was twelve and my mother didn't yet trust me enough to leave me home alone for an afternoon, she took me to her TOPS Club meeting. TOPS stood for "Take Off Pounds Sensibly," a support group originally founded in 1948 in Milwaukee, Wisconsin. There was a diet plan, but there was also a focus on not letting idle hands be the devil's workshop—my mother started doing childish arts and crafts as some attempt to avoid snacking after dinner. I used to admire this rainbow she fashioned with a plastic frame and multicolored ribbons, little plastic beads hanging from the ends. "Don't touch that," she'd tell me. "It's not a toy." *Well, I'm twelve and this is a craft made out of ribbons and beads, so what the fuck is it?* My mother still has it hidden in a junk drawer; I still want it and I don't know why.

For a year, my mom attended weekly meetings at the Cedarbrae Community Center, where she'd sit in a circle with other middle-aged women to talk about her week. "This week, I *turtled*," she said, which I later found out meant she had neither lost nor gained, a victory unto itself. The women clapped modestly. I went to that meeting at a time of my childhood where I knew inherently my weight was a "problem" for a lot of people but I didn't yet feel like it was a problem for me. I was uncomfortable with my body but only because everyone around me kept reacting to how much it was changing. As soon as I had a handle on it, a new cup size would pop up, a new dimple of cellulite, a new inch of soft flesh around my midsection. My mother would see my new additions in a changing room or when she walked into my bedroom without knocking, holding piles of my clean laundry.

I came to that TOPS meeting dressed up: my favorite stretchy jeans, the ones with the ruched waist that never dug into my skin, a Coca-Cola cap, a gray T-shirt, and my puffy red vest. I even wore my good black socks, the ones where the seam didn't needle into the tips of my toes, slowly driving me insane with every step. This was the height of fashion. I had recently cut almost all my hair off and decided I was a tomboy, which was a strange choice for a young girl who sincerely loved glitter and dress-up. It was a clear defense mechanism after I convinced myself that I was not beautiful and so it was in my best interest to remove any doubt about it. I was a tough girl now, and so it was athletic vests and ironic ball caps for me. There was no way I'd give someone an opportunity to even *think* that I considered myself attractive. I chewed gum throughout my mom's meeting and waited for it to end.

An older woman approached my mother on our way out. She and I were at least forty years apart and around the same size—she had no visible pounds to lose, sensibly or otherwise, and yet here she was, talking about cottage cheese with salsa and rice cakes with low-fat peanut butter. She touched my shoulder gently while looking at my mother. "Your son is so cute," she said, reaching an arm out and squeezing my bicep. My mother shrieked with laughter and pushed me into her breast. "This is my *daughter*!" she said, near tears about how funny this was. I was mortified: My weight felt like a direct connection to my lack of femininity. I was less of a girl the more body I had. Here, my worst fears were validated.

My own agita aside, this felt like a more innocent time of my mom's weight-loss attempts, when she was able to laugh about her efforts and also maybe sneak in a low-cal mint chip ice cream bar. It was in the next ten years that her diets curled around her like a vise. Did she even want to escape them? Or was it the only place she felt safe anymore, in the guarantee that she was doing the good, female work of trying to shrink herself ever smaller?

———

My mother dragged herself through every diet conceivable. She did Weight Watchers and Jenny Craig (she contests the latter but the guidebooks that littered our home tell a different story). She went low carb and high fat. She increased her protein and then cut down her sugars. One diet left her so nutrient deficient she had to go to the doctor for weekly shots to make sure she didn't succumb to scurvy. I hated that diet the most: her moodiness became sharp and sudden. Sometimes she'd be crying on the couch, in grief over her parents who had died a few years earlier, or because she had gone through my diary and read something unsavory like, "when will a boy finally rail me in the way I, a blossoming woman, deserve?" But sometimes she would be so angry that I would search for new places to hide. In my closet, I cleared a few things out and put down my baby blanket, some comfort toys, a notebook, and a flashlight. I was fifteen, too old to be looking for cool, arid places to hide from my own mother like a nervous lizard, but I liked hiding in there when she was too sharp to hug.

At my brother's wedding, she ate so little, trying to winnow herself down to a smaller size, that she fainted during one of the ceremonies. No one stopped the events; they just fanned her and offered her orange juice until she came back to the surface.

"You know how your mom is," one of my cousins told me, as if self-torture is more acceptable if it is routine. I was at my thinnest at that wedding; I knew, because my mom told me I was. She was proud. I was hungry.

———

So I know very well where this starts. I know it comes from magazines and television and actresses and cruel comments at school and standard sizing at clothing stores that make you feel bad about being in the double digits, as if that means anything at all, and denim companies that size down, escalating the struggle to fit into a pair of knock-off Levi's with no stretch. I know it comes from the way my dad prized thinness, his own being such a victory despite his inherent inability to gain weight. Or it comes from the bucket seating on the subway which tells me exactly how large they think my ass should be, or maybe it comes from porn, where women's bodies never fold into mounds, they just curl and curve, stomachs flat, like lithe, hairless cats. Or maybe from my ex-husband, who told me innocently enough that I had the widest rib cage of any woman he had ever slept with, a sentence that sent me into a tailspin of googling "average ribcage woman" for weeks, or when he told me that my bulimia was "a teenager's affliction" after he caught me vomiting in the bathroom of his apartment after dinner. But then again, it might be the women I've been around all my life who've bonded with me and with each other by comparing diets and rules, like how "I don't eat bread" is a normal statement in these circles, or maybe "I'm not doing sugar right now," as if sugar is a hobby that you can take or leave depending on how busy you are that month. Or the women who were friends with my ex-husband's friends, women I don't see anymore, who didn't care for me in their group because I was too young and too ethnic and too loud, and I always made jokes about their husbands having small dicks (in my defense, they wouldn't have gotten so angry if it weren't true). They retaliated by telling me they had some clothes they were getting rid of but, "Oh, you know, they might be too small for you," and then begging me to try them on anyway, because watching me get stuck in a blouse—real women call their shirts blouses—would be the night's real show.

I know where it starts. I know where it comes from. What I'd like to find out is when it stops.

⚡

My nutritionist was a skeletal woman from New Jersey named Jackie, whose office was a few minutes from mine in midtown, and who I visited every few weeks for the two worst years of my marriage. Her office was always roiling with heat—one of the side effects of being thin, according to thin people, is that they're always cold, but as a non-thin person, sitting in her office felt like standing on the surface of the sun. She pulled out props to demonstrate portions, like a deck of cards to indicate how much protein you need on your plate at dinnertime. Her filing cabinet was covered in little kitschy faux-retro magnets with images of fifties house-wives and taglines that said things like, "The couch is a no eating zone" and "Step away from the fridge!" and "Nothing tastes as good as HEALTHY feels." I liked her, for some reason. When her mother called, her ringtone changed from a typical *brrr*ing to the sound of a squawking chicken. I knew it was her mother because she told me, with a bitter little laugh, before she turned the ringer off and dumped the phone at the bottom of what sounded like an empty metal drawer that went straight to the pits of hell.

Our appointments were half an hour long, and all I ever did was tell her what I had been eating. Chicken tacos with too much hot sauce. Avocado toast even though I hate avocados. Cottage cheese with salt and pepper. Helen Rosner's Roberto stew from *The New Yorker* with homemade garlic bread. Chicken caesar salad but I only had half of it. Tofu. Six peanuts. For weeks, she wouldn't let me have any sugar; she said it takes twenty-one days to break an addiction. I usually made it thirty days before giving in, and then I would start all over again. I'm not sure what was supposed to happen after the month was up. Whenever I asked her, she'd just counsel me to begin anew.

I began going to Jackie right after I moved to New York and my bingeing started up again, pronounced and shameful. My ex-husband would hear me sometimes, as my esophagus isn't much quieter than the rest of me after all, and we'd have a fight and I'd promise never to do it again. My nails started peeling again from the acids in my stomach rushing back up to my mouth. I could smell vomit on myself all the time, which made me think everyone else probably could too. I got canker sores and burst blood vessels in my eyes. It was embarrassing, and my mind gravitated to the same thought: I'm too old for this.

I never found Jackie helpful. In fact, she made me feel worse about myself when she made me feel anything at all. Jackie never asked me how stressed out I was about work, where, by the way, I was being threatened with a lawsuit for what felt like the thirtieth time because of an article I wrote about a pseudo-doctor on television. She never asked what my marriage was like, just about the meals that my husband and I shared. "What do you eat together at dinner?" she asked me.

I glowed in response, because *this* I could answer. "Big bowls of spaghetti and meatballs. Boeuf bourguignon in the winter. Mussels in the summer. Bún thịt nuong made from scratch. Wild rice bowls with spinach and sausage. Asparagus risotto. Paella, he even bought a special pan for it. Shrimp tacos with cabbage slaw. Beef Wellington on my birthday." My ex-husband loved to cook, and he fed me well from the moment we met. I gained weight steadily when we were together, and sometimes I felt admiration for the addition. *This is love*, I thought, looking at the clothes that no longer fit. Someone loved me so much they wanted to fill me to the brim. "Slow-barbecue ribs. Black pepper beef. Green curry with brown rice. Zucchini noodles with chicken cutlets. Lamb shanks. Turkey burgers."

Jackie shook her head disapprovingly when I told her how much my husband loved me. Jackie knew I had an eating disorder, but she still had me count my calories and, above all, my carbs. "You can't have bread every day," she told me, when I was very much eating bread every day. "It sounds like your husband is a nice cook, but that's not sustainable forever."

After a few months, I stopped seeing Jackie because there was no way for me to explain to her that I couldn't live without eating his food. His cooking was the only way he showed me affection anymore. I didn't yet know what to make of the fact that he watched what I put on my plate, that he had an eye on how much love I filled myself with. He fed me all the time, but it was a trap. How was I supposed to fill myself up with the one thing he gave me without my body showing the difference? I wanted to stay tight and small for him, but I only felt that he loved me when I presented myself in the kitchen for dinnertime. I didn't want to be selfish, but I also didn't want Jackie to take away what little I could shovel up with my fork.

I miss Jackie sometimes. I liked her rules because they were clear. I failed them, but they were clear.

⚡

My eating disorder promised to help me disappear. I wanted to vanish. That's what everyone says about their attempts to starve themselves. But such is the irony of hurting yourself: everyone can see it, everyone can tell, and everyone is waiting for you to perk up and see it, too.

During the lockdown, I called my friend Barb to catch up. We tried our best to re-create over Zoom what our time together might've been like in person: a few glasses of wine, Barb lighting enough candles to give me an arson-related nightmare later that night, some mild to medium gossip about people we hadn't seen in four years. On this particular night, Barb wanted to play a card game called We're Not Really Strangers, which is less of a "game" and more of what I would call "an exercise in testing exactly how much witchcraft I'll allow in my life." Every round, Barb would pull a card that asked a ridiculous and wildly intimate question—"What was your first impression of me?" or "Do you think I've ever had my heart broken?" or "What can I teach you?" I want to be clear: if anyone other than Barb so much as suggested playing this game, I would have immediately called the police despite being an abolitionist. Do you realize how much I have to love you in order to play a card game that asks, earnestly, "What character do you think I would play in a movie?" We all know it's going to be whomever Mindy Kaling is playing that year. It's fine. We don't need to make a whole meal out of this answer.

But for Barb, I did it anyway. I've known Barb for sixteen years, and can't think of a safer place for my anxieties and insecurities. She is a vault for my failures. We knew the answers for most of the questions we asked each other, until near the end when I was forced to ask her, "What do you think is my biggest weakness?"

Barb didn't even flinch. "Your looks," she said, which made me feel like someone had poured hot oil into my ears. "I don't mean you're not attractive. I mean that it's clear that you feel like you're not attractive. It's just obvious that you're not really comfortable with how you look, and *you* feel like it's your weakness."

I've been embarrassed a lot in my life. I once walked into the boys' bathroom during the mandatory swim classes we had at school, resulting in me seeing the first three penises I'd see in my life (I have since seen many, *many* more). I've confused two of the same white, brunette, 5'2" coworkers several times in a row. I have thrown up in cabs in four major American metropolises. The thought of a particular Nike store in New England still makes me nauseous after I barfed on it the morning following a Red Sox game, red Gatorade painting the outside of a heritage building. But this assessment from Barb felt like someone had peeled off a layer of my skin, exposing my most intimate parts, like my feelings were written on the underside of my flesh. How did Barb know? I thought—for my whole life, for the entirety of my relationship with her—that I was doing a good job hiding it. And with the precision of a child raised on Operation, she stretched her hand toward my chest, the constellation of moles on her forearm mocking me, and plucked out my darkest secret, my little shame, the self-terror I tortured myself with for decades. Then she held it in front of my face and said, *I found this. It's yours, right? You talk about it all the time so surely it must be yours.*

"Oh," I said, hoping that maybe this time I would get lucky and all that lightning my mother once threatened me with would finally hit my apartment, electrocuting me and freeing me from this conversation. "I guess I was hoping no one noticed I felt that way about myself. It feels so petty."

Barb shrugged, her surgery on my feelings commonplace to her. "That's the hope, right?" she said. "That your friends can see you in the places you go to hide."

That night was years ago now. Some things are different— we're no longer in isolation, no longer forced to have pathetic facsimiles of time together through Zoom—and others are the same. But I can so viscerally feel the humiliation of her answer. I wasn't hiding at all; in fact, my eating disorder had consumed so much of my life that it was now a defining characteristic. I wasn't simply a woman with *weird vibes* around diet and exercise; I was a woman whose thoughts took the simple form of *calories in, calories out.*

Growing older means finding out you're fucking things up in brand-new ways. When I was sixteen, I was a failure because I thought I was fat. In my late twenties, I became a failure because I thought I was fat *and* because I knew better than to think being fat was a problem in the first place. I read books by women with active eating disorders and ones by women who claimed to be long healed. I read books by fat-positive nutritionists and body-neutrality activists. I read about real fatphobia—how it prevents fat people from getting work or boarding an airplane with a modicum of dignity—and about how mid-sized and thin women perpetrate a war against all our bodies through our anxiety about becoming fat ourselves. I read about disability and health and diabetes and heart disease and the racist history of the body-mass index.

It is much easier to hate your body when you refuse to see it within a continuum of oppression. For so long, hating our bodies was viewed as a private, necessary act of self-loathing. It was important to keep ourselves in check. But if you view it as a larger societal failure—like anti-Blackness or littering or literally anything that happens in an American post office—then it behooves you to adjust your thinking. You are no longer ruining your own life, you're ruining someone else's. Your ideology is contagious.

Self-loathing is transmissible through the air. We can't truly hate our bodies without hating anyone in a body larger than ours. There's no ambivalence on this, no wiggle room. Any attempt to lose weight purely for aesthetic reasons is, ultimately, fatphobia weaponized. Just because you point a gun to your own head doesn't make it less of a gun; it doesn't mean someone else can't pick it up and then use it on themselves. You have to accept that you're not uglier than anyone, but you're not more beautiful. That your body isn't just something to be admired—though it can be, if you want—but a tool that lifts, moves, twists, breaks, folds, and dies. It requires the radical act of no longer comparing yourself to your friends, the radical act of loving yourself so you can love everyone who doesn't look like you, too. It means you have to think beyond your own pain and the cruelty you learned to dig at yourself with.

Do I really think that *everyone* should torture themselves over their body just because I have? Do I really think that anyone with a body bigger than mine should feel as bad as I do? I want joy for other people. Can I start with myself? When we were roommates, Barb would sometimes speak so cruelly about her own body that it made me think she had cognitive issues. She picked at parts of herself that I didn't even notice, or more often ones I had admired. We were close enough that she and I would change our clothes in front of each other, and I liked seeing her body unfiltered, the way I admired my older cousins when they got ready for weekends out when I was five or six years old. How could she hate this? To me, she was shaped like sanctuary.

Could I give myself some grace as a way to give it to Barb? Don't I want that for her?

↯

It was not lost on me that as soon as I left my husband, my father started talking about my appearance again. Sometimes it was small: "You look tan," he'd say after I took a brief trip to Las Vegas to see BTS with my niece, our hormones pumping, making her feel like a real woman and me feel like a little girl.

But soon, it was cruelty wrapped in faux concern. "When are you back in New York?" he asked me when I FaceTimed from a business trip on the West Coast. "You need to see a doctor." He motioned to his own neck, forming a claw with his fingers to indicate that I had some lump where my carotid artery lay. He had said this to me a few times, but never while I was married—the appearance of married women was always the domain of their husbands, he believed. As soon as the women of the family became the property of another man, his right to cast aspersions on our looks—an otherwise routine device deployed against us—ended with the legal document's signature.

But now, I was his again. There were and are so many ways he didn't think I could take care of myself, and supposedly this was another one. Pre-marriage, the *circumference* of my body parts was always an issue. When I was twenty-one, he gasped as I walked through the entryway of the living room. "Your arms," he said, marveling at me like I was a dinosaur brought to life. "They are . . . unmanageable." His fixation on my neck was decades-long; he always thought I had a thyroid condition, making it swollen and enlarged. For most of my life, I've looked at my neck and considered it an enemy combatant on my body. Papa talked about it like the creature from *Alien* was liable to burst out of my skin any minute.

My mother tried to soften the blow: "Don't be sensitive," she said. "He's just worried that you have a goiter." I repeated the words to myself, agog at how it was being presented like a comfort: *He's just worried that you have a goiter.* Like all I needed was an iodine smoothie.

My mom's attitude on weight and diet has changed drastically in the last decade. When I texted her about TOPS recently, she didn't dwell on the year she spent picking at herself in her meetings and instead asked, "What's the name of that frozen treat at Dairy Queen?"

"A Blizzard?" I said. "Why? Do you want one?"

"Yes," she said, in the way that I remember my mom talking about sugar: conspiratorial and giddy. "Badly." Sometimes, when I visit, my mom and I get ice cream. Not a low-fat version. The real shit. I don't let her talk about calories; she has stopped offering to calculate the sin in real time.

It seems like, overnight, my mother stopped caring. She got rid of old clothes that didn't really fit and bought bright clothes in the right sizes. She stopped counting calories and measuring portions. She stopped dyeing her hair and let the soft white grow out from her scalp. She ate an entire brownie that she found in the freezer that turned out to be filled with potent weed, and then proceeded to eat two, maybe three bowls of steaming pasta. She got drunk on FaceTime with me and started talking like a jazz cat from an off-brand kids movie.

"Heyyyyy bayyyybyyyyy," she slurred after half a glass of pissy white wine. "What's goin' oooooon?" She didn't give up; she gave in to what she was supposed to be all along. I like her so much now.

I was proud of my mother for not dieting for my wedding. It was never even on the table. I was especially proud of that restraint after I *left* my marriage—imagine if she had done all that shrinking and shirking for wedding photos, when those photos are now just collecting dust in the darkest recesses of my dank little apartment. I'm glad I didn't diet either, that I didn't work hard to shrink for a day that would one day feel like a sour taste in the back of my throat. I'm forgetting, more and more, what day was actually my wedding day. Was it September 15? 18? It doesn't matter—that anniversary is now just the feeling of someone walking too close to you in the dark. It's the smell of something that's turned in the back of your fridge. It ended so fast, a helpful reminder that I can lose everything in a matter of days. But look: my body is still here.

⚡

Divorce is rough. It's rough on how you perceive yourself. It forces you to look at the body you have after you begin again, again. In the months after I moved out, I traced lines across my neck, pressed my hands against it to make sure my fingers could wrap around, pressed on every fold and fat pocket to see if it was proof of a chronic condition. If I could strangle myself with my own hands, I was beautiful. I pressed my arms against my side and watched them flatten and widen. I hated my arms. My stomach rippled in all the wrong ways. I was soft, moveable, melted, like putty shaped into a crooked cylinder. For the fourth time in ten years, I made another appointment to have my thyroid checked. I knew what they'd say, but I did it anyway; Papa had trained me to believe that anything about my body that diverged from thinness was the cause of illness, disease, or malfunction. Having a fat neck wasn't an acceptable affliction—which is exactly what it was. An affliction. I missed my eating disorder more than I missed my ex-husband. He brought me brief comfort, but bulimia brought me a way to hide. He saw me, all the time, for who I was, until he didn't. By that point, he was gone. My eating disorder, conversely, never let me see myself. It was a shield.

My ex was always feeding me. I want to remember him fondly and so I think of spaghetti squash with sun-dried tomatoes and pesto, cheddar-jalapeño biscuits, the mint chocolates his ex-girlfriend's mother used to send him every Christmas, even after we got married. Then again, I ate whatever he served me: I consumed his version of events always, his side of an argument, his perspective of all matters big and small. I followed his routine and his timelines.

There was never any force; I willingly gobbled up whatever he served. I ate in front of him, greedily and fast and sloppy, and felt loved for it. Finally someone who wants to feed me. I didn't take any time to consider how much bullshit I had to eat in order to finally feel full.

I remember so little of the month after I left my marriage, except for how impossible it felt to eat. Food was always tied to pleasure or punishment, and I wanted neither. I had been punished plenty in my marriage and couldn't take another painfully distended stomach from bingeing or the burn of throwing it up, and I didn't think I deserved any joy at all. But there was an upside to feeling emotionally exterminated. This was the moment I had been waiting for my entire life! The catastrophe that would make me thin! For once, at long last, I didn't want to eat at all. Food was revolting. I was never a very good anorexic; waiting too long to eat was only pleasurable if there was a binge and purge at the end of that cycle. The point of starving myself was to wring out all the pleasure I could from eating, and then banish the evidence from my body as soon as possible. Consumption was ugly to me. Even when my grief was at its worst, when it felt like a thick fog I couldn't see through, when it made me walk into walls and forget my own name and lose track of hours and days and weeks, I greedily thought: Will I emerge from this *skinny*? If that's the result of all this, then at least when people looked at me with their sad Scaachi's-getting-divorced looks, I'd look *good*. No one cares about your turmoil if you're using it as a way to get hot.

I track my life in phases of how much my mother calls me, and during this time, she called three, sometimes four times daily. That's how much trouble I was in; her attention was constant. I never had anything to say and always tried to get off the phone as fast as I could. She asked the questions she always did during our daily calls, but with a renewed urgency. "What did you do today?" turned into "Do you feel safe today?" "Are you going anywhere today?" turned into "Have you gone outside at all today?" "Do you need money?"

turned into "Does he have access to your money?" And nor-mally, my mother would ask if I had eaten, what I had eaten, whether the food had "value"—meaning, if it was healthy, if it would keep me lean, if it would keep me going. That changed after my husband became my ex-husband.

Most days, I languished in a bed that didn't belong to me, in an apartment I was borrowing, ordering food and letting it rot in the fridge because consumption felt excessive. My skin changed color. I was more ashen, my eyes bulged through dark circles. I didn't get thinner but I did get sicker. My body stayed the same shape and size, but I felt so small that if I walked over a subway grate, I'd slip through the cracks like a briny mystery liquid.

Day after day, my mother would call, and request some-thing she never really had before. "I need you to eat," she said. "Eat whatever you can. Make sure you eat a few times a day. Eat anything you want. As long as you eat."

It was the first time in my life that I took her advice with-out even thinking about it. I ate and ate and ate. I never had an appetite, and could only pretend food was still enjoyable, but I was relentless in taking her guidance. I ate rice bowls and noodles and dumplings and dosa and chips and crudités and croissants and cookies. If I had a thought about food, it entered me within moments. I never purged; I let my body swell and ache so I could relearn how to stop when I needed to stop. I let hunger fill me to the brink and then spoke to it with spring rolls crushed in two bites.

My mother started calling me even more, focused on the same question: "Did you eat?" Yes, I'd tell her. I ate plenty. I could almost hear her blood pressure go back down to a nor-mal range. I loved those calls. The food was sometimes healthy, more often not, but it was something. I'd text her pic-tures of empty takeout containers and she'd always text back, immediately, "Good." I used to protest when she'd call and ask what I had for lunch—"Mom, it's 5:25"—but now I rushed to answer the phone so I could hear her give me permission. "Did you eat?" she'd say. "You have to eat. Eat everything. Eat whatever you want. Eat now."

What a risk, to trust my body. I had never listened to it before in my life; now, at my most vulnerable, I did. Why not? What else could I possibly lose? I hadn't gained any-thing from restriction and staying sick. Being careful around carbs and sugars didn't help me "keep" a husband, as if one could be kept anyway, as if they won't just do whatever they gotta do regardless.

But it was a risk, too, to listen to my mother, who had steered me wrong for decades. I listened to her so much, even when she didn't think I was listening. I listened to her pick at herself and restrict herself from so much pleasure and selfish joy. I listened to how she talked about other bodies, and how she talked about my own. I listened to her ruin her own fun, and I learned from her how to ruin mine the older and older I got. But her directives didn't just feel like a worth-while suggestion, they felt like an order. *Eat. Be in your body. Build it back and make it home.*

I have been losing the fight with my own body for a deceptively simple reason: I treat it as a fight in the first place.

But I don't need to hide from myself, or hide myself from other people. Besides, I cannot hide because no one will let me. Even if I try to slink away to an invisible place, someone will come and get me. It's nice in the light if you can stand in it long enough to feel the warmth. Looking at my body with my own gaze is a light unto itself. I try to stay there as much as I possibly can. My mother told me to eat, and so I did.

TWO STARS

My ex-husband loved to tell the same joke about the Canadian-US border: "It's the world's largest one-way mirror. Canadians look down and see Americans, and Americans look up and see themselves." He'd take a long sip of his red wine after he said this, while the people around him at a party in Toronto or New York would laugh with the kind of mirth that only comes with attending grad school. I stole the joke a thousand times while we were married, and since our divorce a thousand times more. I wonder where he first heard it, but that's one of those questions I can't ask him anymore.

I thought about that one-way mirror whenever I read the Goodreads reviews of my first book. Goodreads, a democratized book review website steadily destroyed by people who can't fucking read, wasn't a place I visited often. I don't have an account, and I don't use it myself. I was cautioned against looking at it when I became an author, and so I mostly kept away except for three or four moments of arrogance. *I feel good about myself today*, I thought. *I'm strong enough to read what three thousand strangers have to say about the thing I'm most proud of. I sure hope someone has some specific and unhelpful criticisms for me to never forget for the rest of my creative life!*

A few months after my book came out, I got a two-star review from a familiar name. There was nothing else to it: just two stars, thrown over her shoulder it seemed. I called my then-boyfriend over to my laptop to show him the evidence. "What," I asked him, hand on my hip, my skin on fire, "is this?"

My ex had an ex-girlfriend who seemed to never fully recede from view. They had dated before we did, and I hoped that eventually her presence would no longer be felt. She was smart and beautiful and alabaster and blonde. I had seen her in our old neighborhood in Toronto before; she seemed to walk on air. I was in my early twenties, and she was eight years older than me: she was sexy and mature, with slender arms, and lips that curled up at the corners like she had a secret that she was unwilling to tell me. I hated her, instinctively, spending more than a few days looking at her Facebook, her Instagram, her Twitter, and thinking of all the ways I did not compare.

"You still like her," I had told my boyfriend. "You like that she's white and you wish I were. You like her blonde hair. You like how narrow her body is." I wanted to trap my boyfriend into admitting something I was worried was true—he had access to white people in a way I didn't, and one day he'd return to his own people, his own women. "You're obsessed with her!" I'd cry, my paranoia becoming more and more specific by the minute. "You like how her hips are small enough that she can fit between two chairs at a cramped restaurant! You liked finding her long blonde hairs in your eggs! You miss how you can see her iris and her pupil as distinct elements of her cornea!!!!"

How strange to see her name next to a review on Goodreads. No words, only the two stars, next to her name and her photo. My boyfriend seemed genuinely surprised to see the rating, even while I somehow felt like he was in on this. He hugged me for a while to calm me down and reassured me that I was simply insane. It wasn't a big deal; I was a crazy person, is all.

"Look, even Ernest Hemingway only has a 3.8 on Good-reads," he said. "Do you want me to tell her to delete it?"

I wasn't upset that this woman didn't like my book. She wouldn't have been the first. I had gotten bad reviews before, and I'd had boyfriends with nosy exes before. There was something potent about the way she accessed me on the internet—*my* internet. I had built my career there, my social life, my sense of self. My whole life, it seemed, was wrapped up in the internet, which was wrapped up in my work. I've been writing online since I was fourteen, and so I have been fighting on the internet for the better part of two decades. This was a different kind of fight. I didn't want to have it at all; it seemed uneven from the start. Her work was private, her accounts mostly restricted to me, and I knew far less about her than she knew about me. After all, it was clear she read my book, and so she had read the long version of how my soon-to-be husband and I got together, and how wonderful he was. She knew how much he loved me, and how hard it was for me to accept being loved. She had a front-row view of how much work I put into ensuring my parents loved him like I did. She could see all of me, and I could see only slivers of her, only my most anxious projection, my most pitiful worry. "She's just jealous that things didn't work out between us," my boyfriend—eventually, our ex—told me. He said it like he was the prize, as if I had won something. It bothered me, but then I remembered: I wrote it that way, too.

⚡

Divorce would be easy if you never had to tell anyone about it. When it was clear that there was no way to save our relationship, I spent nights awake thinking about how I would explain to everyone that I couldn't do it anymore. My cousins and brother would be easy, my parents would be impossible, my friends would probably see it coming. But it was the wider public I was worried about, the strangers I talk to on the internet every day. People I half know, or barely know, or don't know at all, who watch what I do on the internet merely because I've invited them to do it. The internet has turned everything into a performance; you can find an audience invested in how you brush your teeth (YouTube vlogs), how well you can lip-sync and dance (TikTok), how you're voting (Facebook), what form your activism takes (Instagram), or even how unbearable you are about the shit you like (Letterboxd). The monotonous is reshaped for public consumption, so naturally, our lives' bigger moments merit the production, too. But in the limited way I perform online, I wasn't sure how to do the divorce announcement dance.

It wasn't just that I had to tell people online, or alert my friends from out of town who'd never know unless I told them the bad (or was it good?) news. My writing has often led a lot of people to think they know me intimately; the best way to tell a story is to tell the listener exactly where you're coming from. They weren't wrong about that, but they weren't right either. My work kept me in my marriage longer than I want to admit. I didn't know how to write about how it was failing; my first book was lousy with details about how well he had treated me, and how good we were together. I believed it; I was one of the last two people on earth who did.

I'm harassed online, routinely—it's just a part of the job. And even though I'm at a point in my life where an internet death threat barely moves the needle (not the sentence I was promised by late-stage capitalistic white millennial digital media feminism, is it!), I felt anxious about the performance of divorce online. My breakup would be used against me by trolls and angry internet readers and anyone who thought I deserved unhappiness. What's the best way to tell people? A press release is lunacy—I'm not a celebrity, but I did appreciate its efficacy. What if I skipped over it entirely, and just talked about myself like I was single, as if my marriage never existed? "Sad clown seeking singles; must love old movies, kitty cats, and gazing into eyes that are perpetually glassy with unexplained tears." But I didn't want to date, not yet. An Instagram announcement also felt flimsy: "We're saddened to announce that after much consideration, we've decided to separate. We make this decision with love and care for one another, and hope to stay close friends through this process. We'd appreciate your privacy during this time." That's not even true! No one was *sad*; he was furious and I had no feelings at all. The decision wasn't made with love for each other, but was simply a survival instinct. We would not be friends. We never really were: the original sin of our doomed union.

Of course, I couldn't even begin to consider the process of posting about my divorce online until I told people in my tangible life first. Telling my father was a specific nightmare that I'm glad I'll never have to relive, his ruddy face looking at me perplexed over FaceTime, asking if he should fly to New York to "get me," whatever that meant. My friends were told through a few well-placed texts to notorious gossips; that would do most of the work for me. Initially I tried to find some fun in the way I told people, like when my friend Sarah chirped me on Valentine's Day during a podcast recording.

"Scaachi, what's it like to be loved on Valentine's Day?" she said.

"I don't know, Sarah," I said. "I'm getting a divorce."

Her face froze when she realized I wasn't kidding (as did the four other people on the call, none of whom knew me at all). It was the first time I had laughed since my husband stopped being my husband. We were still living together at the time, still half in a pandemic.

I used to record the podcast in our walk-in closet (another casualty of our marriage—god, to stand *in* a closet, what a luxury I had), and when I emerged, he perked up. "What was so funny?" he asked. "I could use a laugh, too."

"Oh, you know," I said. "You just had to be there."

After my marriage ended, I lost protection in ways I never imagined. Men treated me wildly differently. In person, they were so much sweeter. They looked at my left hand, saw the absence of a ring, and opened doors for me with a big smile. Men who were my friends started complimenting me on my looks, replying to my Instagram stories, trying to weasel their way into an invite to my new apartment. (It never worked, and will never work. If we are friends, it is simply because I find you at least somewhat repulsive, by design.) Online, they were crueler about my weight and my looks, more direct about how my divorce happened because my husband clued in that I was ugly and fat and annoying. Those comments made me laugh; I wished it had been so simple as just being my fault.

Once you commit to monogamy, the gossip potential around you shrinks. In divorce you watch it engorge again, your potential for being the center of a story ever increasing. Once I started talking about my divorce online, strangers online were intent to find out the big Ws: why, when, and who's keeping the cat.

Strangers with their verifiable names connected to their profiles asked me about my divorce, but then again, so did complete strangers hiding in the shadows. Within weeks of

my separation, I started to get anonymous messages prob-
ing me for more details about my split. I could never get a
handle on the demographics of the person sending them—or
people, there was always enough of them that I considered
a small army may have been responsible—but whoever it was
had created a flawed and disappointing version of me in their
head. They messaged me about how I was a self-loathing
brown person, and that's why I married a white guy (6/10,
decent argument but needs more detail). They messaged me
about how I hung out with too many white people (3/10,
they're just the losers I've met in newsrooms, take it up with
the hiring committee). They told me that I spent too much
time in my work catering to white people (2/10, read the
room, sweetie). They begged me, for my next sexual act, to
date a brown man instead (0/10, have you *met* a brown man,
what exactly do you think that'll fix for me?).

I think about my original sin a lot, my choice to start
writing about myself in the early 2010s, during the personal
essay boom that mellowed into the culture essay boom of
the mid-2010s and now, in the mid-2020s, is something
more like the personality-driven content-creator market. I
wrote about myself because I was really good at it; people
kept telling me as much. And—this is an important factor
that a lot of writers and performers don't admit to enough—
I liked the attention. I would likely not make a good actor
because I want credit for being interesting enough as myself.
I'd never be a good editor because I like how warm a spot-
light feels. Praise for my abilities is all very fine and good,
but I want people to tell me it's nice to spend a few hundred

pages with me. I allowed myself to be my work when I should have protected myself better. It's like I intentionally built my house on a tilt, and now I'm complaining that all my drinks keep sliding off my table, crashing into the walls.

The risks were greater than what I understood in my teens, when I first started writing personal essays. I thought the worst thing that could happen is someone would mis-understand me, that my message wouldn't get across, that people wouldn't *like* me or the work. That was shortsighted, the perspective of a young woman who hadn't had her heart shattered like a windshield. The greatest risk is that people would understand me perfectly well. There's nowhere to hide in writing. You just have to let yourself be visible, and trust that your reader sees you with compassion and care. I've regretted, a thousand times, letting anyone into my inner sanctum like that. Now, I'm trapped: To write about my divorce is to give more of myself at a time when I feel like I already have so little. To not write about it is a conspicuous omission, one that feels insincere, incomplete, and inaccurate.

But look, it's not like anyone handled hearing about it in per-son that well either. "SCAACHI," screamed my former boss when I saw him in Toronto years after I got married, moved, got divorced, and then visited for the first time. "CAN I BUY YOU A SHOT?"

His volume would have been more appropriate for an air-raid siren, an interesting turn for someone who's generally so soft-spoken. When we worked together, I felt like I had to stand on his toes with my ear directly in his mouth to hear his edits. "Are you offering because you feel bad about my life?" I asked.

"NO!" he yelled. "OR, WELL, YES. MAYBE. I DON'T KNOW. DO YOU WANT A SHOT OR WHAT?"

Reader, I wanted a free shot.

Others were much worse, like the man who patted me on the shoulder at a party after not having laid eyes on me for a full decade. He used to circle parties attended by eighteen-to twenty-one-year-old journalists, mostly students trying to find a crack in. He was a big crack. "I heard about your divorce," he said, apparently believing this was an appropriate greeting to replace *hello*.

"Yes," I said.

"That sucks," he said.

"It does," I said.

"Are you . . . okay?" he asked. People asked me this specific question all the time, and I never knew what answer they were hoping for. "Yes" felt unbelievable; if I told them the truth, it would be too intimate and cloying.

People looked—and still look—at me with their big, wet eyes. I know they want to ask what happened but they know they can't; the ones bold enough to ask are broken people who have no sense of what public humiliation feels like. When my colleague asked me if anyone in my marriage cheated, I felt like a piece of machinery malfunctioning after someone poured sand into its gears. I stuttered and sputtered something about *no, of course not*, and spent the rest of the meeting wondering if everyone else was thinking the same thing.

The only person who handled news of my divorce particularly well was my friend Rudy, who bypasses most relationships in order to spend more time being gay, getting tattoos, and hoisting barbells over his head.

"Ooh, a divorcée?" he said outside a whiskey bar in Manhattan, sucking on the end of a Camel Light. "How *louche*."

"I wouldn't say this feels very glamorous at present," I told him.

"Maybe not now. But think of the future!" he said, tossing his cigarette into the street. "Finally, there's something interesting about you."

A lot of people whisper "so young" to themselves—or sometimes they yell it, right at me—when I tell them I'm divorced. This, maybe, is the one I hate the most, because I'm acutely aware that one day, I won't seem like a young divorcée, I'll be an appropriate age to be a divorcée. At forty-seven, people will assume my husband left me during our shared midlife crisis, when in reality, my marriage stripped me raw and left me alone, yet painfully visible, when I was thirty-one. "You have your whole life ahead of you!" one woman told me over drinks. Everyone thinks that a divorce is something to correct, and that because I had so much time to remarry, my life was not yet over. But hearing that just made me tired. I did—do—have my whole life ahead of me, but thinking about the life I've already had makes my limbs stiffen like I'm getting the flu.

Just three months after my husband and I split up, I implemented a rule for strangers: You can ask me about my divorce if you tell me about yours. If your marriage has not ended, alas, you cannot apply. If your partner died, sorry to hear, but do not tell me that story. Divorces only. Tit for tit. I only wanted to talk to people who understood the specific hurt I was swimming in. I was fed up with people trying to approach me with the common ground of "I've never been divorced but a guy on Bumble ghosted me after I told him I wear jeans in bed."

People on the internet are much harder to control when it comes to inappropriate comments. It's impossible to steer the topic of conversation away from your own discomfort when someone starts a conversation in your inbox with, "what happened with you and your husband?" or "did you get a divorce?" or—this one really fucked me up—"you HAVE to tell us what happened!" This kind of communication has always been one way, but usually in the form of strangers speaking to me without reciprocation. Now, they wanted information from me. They wanted engagement.

I *have* to tell them what happened? That's what everyone seemed to be suggesting, stranger or friend alike, and some said it outright. I had an obligation to tell them the entire story before I had processed it myself. I *owed* something to all these witnesses, strangers sitting in front rows of the performance I invited them to. My mother demanded I give her every ugly, sticky detail of what went wrong in my marriage. She wanted me to walk her through it, day by day. It's not that she didn't believe me or that she needed proof that a divorce was the right choice; it was more that she wanted to suffer *with* me so that I wouldn't have to bear it without help. "You shouldn't do it alone," she told me. "I'm your mother. When you're in pain, I'm in pain. So let me be in pain with you."

But recounting the details was agony, not to mention steadily spoiling the few good memories I had left.

Some friends soured on me when I refused to give details; one friend began calling other people, asking them why I wasn't confiding in her about my divorce, asking if I had been canceling dinners and parties because I was avoiding her specifically, and not just every living person in a one-hundred-block radius. Everyone's sense of self became completely outsized, as if they could've somehow cured my ex and me of divorce by being a little more present in our business.

But—and here's the true freak-show side of this—if people didn't ask, *I felt desperate to talk about it.* It was like I was going to parties holding a bat in my mouth, and I couldn't get over how people weren't asking me about the bat. "I have a bat in my mouth! Ask me about the bat in my mouth!" I wanted to scream about my divorce, all day and in public. I felt like I owed everyone an answer, but above all, I owed myself the real estate to talk about it constantly. I rarely went into details, and I never demanded people take my side— though obviously they *should*—but I needed people to remark on how truly bonkers it was that I was getting a divorce, something half of the North American population has done and will do. But no: for me, it was unprecedented, and it needed to be discussed as much as possible, but only on my terms, and only when I wanted to, and only if I wasn't asked.

———

Strangers left comments on my Instagram posts asking where I had moved to, where my apartment was, what happened to my old place in a different, posher, whiter neighborhood in Brooklyn. They asked for my exact coordinates, both physical and emotional. They sent me messages after they put the threads together and wanted to know the *why* of everything. They knew men they could set me up with, if I just answered this DM and told them that yes, of course I'd love to meet their cousin who lives in Ronkonkoma.

The vaguest of acquaintances, people I hadn't heard from since long before I even met my ex-husband, sent me emails asking if they could help. "Scaachi, I just heard the news," they said, as if I had miscarried a full adult man and not simply accepted my fate as a divorced person. "If there's anything I can do, let me know."

I should have started asking for money, but instead I repeated a refrain that became almost biblical to me: "If you found out because I'm joking about it, don't worry. The traumatic part is already long over." It was true on some days; mostly, I didn't want to have to admit again and again to my own vulnerabilities. Yes, I needed a shot. Yes, I needed a ride home. Yes, I could handily find a way to laugh about this, my most cursed life event (so far).

What all these people had in common was how utterly ill-equipped they were to deal with any answer whatsoever. Any response I gave to the probing, on or offline, had to somehow be stoic but not morose, funny without being too cutting, short without being withholding. I still don't know how to do that. I was either too sour, like when a talent agent messaged me asking what led to my divorce. "What compelled you to think it is normal to ask a stranger something like this?" I asked. I did not read her six replies. Or I was too funny, like when I told our newsroom's lawyer about the few weeks I had taken off. "I got Covid, my mom got a knee replacement, but then it got a lot better: I got a divorce!" I slapped him on the arm and he looked at me like I had recently returned from war.

"Oh my god," he said. "No."

"Yes," I reassured him. "Yes."

In a few months, I would be dismissed from this job, alongside everyone else I worked with. The news would get bleaker, and I would get funnier.

But online, in particular, it felt like I was constantly breaking the news to someone, and I knew it was my fault. I had to tell people because I had told them about the first part of the story. I started it! I chose a career path, and ultimately a way of life, that was public and inherently attention-seeking. For a while, the worst thing you could have called me as a memoirist, especially a female one, was navel-gazing. Now, I think the worst thing you can call me is sincere. I'm exhausted from telling the truth all the time. No one really asked me to do it, but now I'm in so deep, I don't even know how I would ever get out.

⚡

Every day, for months, I was reminded of my old life online at every goddamn turn. It was like a *Black Mirror* episode. I kept running into something painful and screaming, "ARE YOU FUCKING KIDDING ME" at my phone while taking one of my little working-from-home-depression walks. Our marriage was plainly laid out in screenshots and emails and texts and Instagrams. Almost every fight we've ever had exists on a server somewhere. Every grandiose pain I've felt about my marriage lives in a folder on my phone's photo app, a carousel of each spider crack in our foundation. If I wanted to feel sad, I had data for it.

First, I went through my Twitter account. I searched for every time I mentioned "my husband" by that term, every time I claimed ownership over him and brought in an audience to witness it. "This is my husband," I was saying over and over and over again. "I love him and he loves me and our hope is to be together until one of us dies." That's what you're saying whenever you telegraph your marriage status. You're telling the people in your orbit that you're *that* sure about something. I used to feel uncomfortable around brides for that reason—they always looked at me with this beatific smile, as if they knew something I didn't and were dying to fill me in. Once I got married, I don't remember ever having that look. I remember feeling like an imposter, like everyone could see the part of my mask where it lifted from my real skin. "Scaachi, do not marry this man," my friend joked to me in a tweet seven years ago. She told me not to marry him because he wanted to buy an ugly hat; like everything, hindsight gives meaning to the meaningless.

I tweeted more about being a wife than I remembered. My writing would've taken such a different shape had my relationship worked; I wonder how I would've reflected on my love of getting in an argument. I'd probably be much more delighted to answer strangers' questions about my most complex human relationship.

"my baby boomer husband is upset that i know michael jordan from space jam and not the nineteen eighty five bulls," I wrote in 2020. That one was okay. Maybe you had to be there.

"legally and morally obligated to end the day by telling you all that the loser husband made me dinner," I wrote the next year, alongside a photo of this fish and lentil dish he made. I always loved it. Sometimes it makes me miss the shape of his neck, so I don't eat it much anymore.

"I would rather die than publicly acknowledge my husband," I said in 2022, a *joke* delivered two months before we'd separate.

I spent so much time thinking about how my own work, my own writing, my own acknowledgment of being a wife had shaped the public perception of me. It made people think they knew me because they knew what my relationship looked like, how it made ripples. I did it on purpose, but it was *my* choice. I never thought much about what kind of trail I was leaving behind, and never considered the impact on anyone else in my life. My husband hated that I wrote about my life and, by extension, his. But, why? Did he resent the profile I was giving him? Was he embarrassed by me and my (several, loud, polarizing) internet public antics? Did it hurt his feelings when I called him a loser in public? I was kidding, like I'm always fucking kidding, but it probably sucked to be the target of my jokes. He probably told me it sucked and I probably didn't listen. The internet is a record of my failures in so many ways, but none more blatant than how the person I loved most in the world and I failed each other. I am tired of the negotiation I make, every day, whether to be my true self online or not. I am tired of wondering whether the record could turn on me eventually or not. What am I so worried about? I'm *dying*. We all are.

My own Instagram bothered me the most. When we separated, I had over two thousand Instagram posts. Most were of my friends, of myself when I felt good (god, remember feeling good?), and of my pet, Sylvia Plath The Cat The First, a rotten little animal who deserves all the salmon in the world. But punctuated among my photos were reminders of the life I had for a little while there. I saw my ex-husband all over my own feed and it infuriated me. One morning, I woke up to a photo on my algorithm from a friend of my ex's. He was visiting New York with his son, and the photo showed my ex giving them the New York tour with his new girlfriend, to the same places we would go with our visiting friends. Now he was going to them with a woman whose name sounded like an Easy-Bake Oven model. She also had blue eyes and blonde hair and narrow hips. She looked like his ex-girlfriend. What can I say? He had a type, but it wasn't me.

My account, meanwhile, was a gravesite to a life I'd lost. Instagram has a functionality to mass-delete, but it didn't work on my phone despite my countless attempts to use it. Everything is an allegory, as ever, so I had to do it manually.

I wiped out any photo that reminded me that nothing had turned out the way I wanted it to. A photo of my hand holding a book, my ruby engagement ring blinging in the corner, gone. Photos of us together, happy and smiling, obliterated. Trips we took together were the most painful, so I erased them all as if they had never happened: Vietnam, Thailand, Greece, Cuba, Mexico, England, Tanzania. The photo of my nails I took in the Uber to our first attempt at couple's therapy—robin's-egg blue and short because my nails kept breaking during that year of life. All our wedding photos. Anything from our engagement party. A photo of the paperback edition of *Infinite Jest*. (This had nothing to do with him, but it was a stupid thing to post, so may as well delete that, too.) Birthday gifts and birthday posts. New Year's Eve 2014. A photo of us at a dinner, which I captioned, "We fight a lot but it's okay." It would not be okay, turns out. Our old apartment. Remember when he would make eggs Benedict on a Saturday? Remember how warm and sure your life felt? Look at this internet time capsule that mocks you. I went so far back I found photos of just his hands, reading Twitter when it was still called that, on a fucking BlackBerry Bold 9650.

Among the most unsettling finds was a snapshot of a Post-it note, a quote from him: "I want to spend the rest of my life struggling for comfort with you." He used to repeat the line to me all the time—sometimes about how he had to tug the blanket away from me while we slept, sometimes about how uncomfortable I made him with my painfully public self. I always thought it was romantic, but now I'm not sure. Should it be a struggle? Does *everything* have to be a fight? I laid out our argument in writing for a decade, and now, I wasn't so sure any of it was worth it. He had been saying the quiet part out loud since the beginning of our relationship. Being with me would be a struggle. To do it, you had to love it. I would and will bring anyone into the public with me. Who could blame him for not wanting such discomfort, forever.

It took me a whole day of intermittent swiping, the app crashing every three deletions I made, before I felt finished. From 2,594 posts, I was whittled down to 983. Of course, all that number did was give me another way to quantify my sadness. I had deleted 62 percent of my posts from the last twelve years; 62 percent of my last eleven years, of effectively my entire life after I left my teens. More than half of my life was disposable, a problem to bury. I wonder if anyone noticed my public record becoming slimmer overnight. I wonder if there are people still looking for photos of us together online because for a long time, googling my name brought his name up, too. I had exposed so much, I wanted to obliterate the record. I didn't want strangers to access my archive of good memories turned bad. I destroyed that record for my own self-preservation, knowing I was destroying the narrative I'd written for others, too. I had given us a good ending, but was now attempting to reverse course. It was a tall order after leaving such a long trail in the opposite direction. All I've done for my entire life, personally and professionally, is make a record. All I've done is leave evidence. All I've done is tell everyone, anyone, everything.

Well. Almost.

✦

The thing my ex hated the most about me was how much I gave to people we didn't even know. "Don't write about this," he'd grumble softly to me after he did something embarrassing at a party or after his body betrayed him on a vacation— happens to the best of us, and I never had plans to go into detail on whatever dysentery opera was ruining his life that given week.

But once we were divorced, it decomposed into something much crueler for me to contend with. "You gotta stop making bank off people," he texted me one day, worried I would write a book entirely about our divorce. (Whoops! But also: Who makes money off . . . books? In 1868's *Little Women*, Jo makes $300 on her book, which is about as much as I expect to make from this book in 2025.) He resented the idea that my narrative might trump his in the public, online sphere where I lived the most. He threatened me with libel and slander suits, nonspecific claims that I was lying about how our relationship fell apart. "You're not going to tell my story."

This was more of the same: our stories had merged, an ownership he liked when we were together but resented once I was able to tell others the same story without his unsolicited edits and unhelpful additions. He was perpetually paranoid that I was going to flame him in a book. I understand why. "You own everything that happened to you," Anne Lamott wrote in her 1994 book *Bird by Bird*. "If people wanted you to write warmly about them, they should have behaved better." A nice concept, even if from a white woman from San Francisco who has blonde dreadlocks and has written *several* books subtitled "Thoughts on Faith."

My ex felt like I was always inviting people into our business, so I was surprised to find out he had invited someone else into our marriage. What am I even supposed to call this woman who left the two-star review? An ex-girlfriend with unfinished business? His paramour? The other woman? None of these words feel quite right. I'll call her Cait instead.

Years after the bad review, after we got engaged and had been married for nearly a year, Cait reared her head one more time. My marriage was rocky by that point, but it was only through Cait that I could identify why. One morning, on Instagram, she sent me a thicket of sixty-nine (*nice*) messages between the two of them, outlining their five-year-long affair. Cait is now the quiet whirr in the background of all my memories with him: She was with us when we got engaged at St. Katharine Docks in London, and on our wedding day in Toronto when my husband held my hands and cheered that "We did it!" and on our honeymoon in Tanzania when we sat down at a romantic dinner on safari, just the two of us, only for our driver to pull up a chair, remarking on the confusing (to him) abundance of rose petals and candles. Cait was in every fight we had, for years—an unknown co-conspirator. She had come with us everywhere we went, all through the little computer my husband carried in his pocket.

It hurt my feelings and made me feel like less of a person,

but there was bonus insult to injury: Did she have to be white? Neither of them seemed to understand why this was a worse crime than the affair itself. Had he cheated on me with Bhumika or Umika or Priyanka or any of the other hot Indian-names-that-end-with-a girlies, I would have been able to understand it more. But with a woman who looked nothing like me, who in fact seemed in total opposition to me? Next time, just fuck each other right on top of my face!

Cheating on me with a white woman seemed like an attempt to eradicate me from the record of my own marriage. So I figured I would do it myself, because it was clear I had the wrong record to begin with. Most of their affair, it was clear, was happening on the internet. On *my* internet. On the very place where my husband told me I was oversharing, where my stories were causing him problems, where he was tired of defending me in feuds and fights. So many strangers had parasocial relationships with me through my writing, but no one more than Cait, who resented that I got the best version of my husband while she got scraps. No one had built a more upsetting narrative about my marriage, and no one had used it against me more. She thought I was happy, and she wanted to make it so I wasn't. There was no way for me to telegraph to her, through my beloved internet, that I was, in fact, perfectly miserable.

"I just don't want you to tell your side of it," my ex-husband said to me after I moved out. I understood his fears, even if I could no longer accommodate them. Though at first I barely told anyone why we were breaking up, I eventually grew tired of keeping all his secrets. For years, I was my ex-husband's safe harbor, and he was mine. We shared our secrets, our worst selves, our ugliest thoughts. He was afraid I'd use it against him and I was worried he'd do the same. I didn't want to ruin his day, or his life, but by the end of our marriage, all I had was that record. The very thing I wanted to obliterate was the only belonging I took from our marriage. Every physical object I took from our apartment, in fact, was in pursuit of writing: The desk where I wrote my internet articles for years. The green chair where I sat slumped over, looking at tweets. The guest bed where I'd sleep on nights we couldn't get along, the internet my company for another night alone.

My ex is the hero of my first book because that's how it felt to me at the time. I felt rescued. It's bad enough to lie to yourself privately, but to sell it to a public who believes those stories, too? It feels like a scam. Strangers are sad to hear about my divorce because they thought my marriage stood for something bigger than just my own relationship. Everyone likes a neat and tidy end to a familiar story you could tell in a thousand different ways. I've always saved my worst self for my private work, the diary I write in nightly. I keep those words to myself; I never even let my ex-husband touch the covers of those journals.

I still struggle with the personal sheddings I leave all over the internet. I've deleted my tweets and my old blog. I don't go out the way I used to. I live alone now, and there's no one to run from in my own home anymore. Writing about yourself for the internet means pulling off little pieces of your body and letting them walk around without you. You have to let them go, and when you meet them again, you might not like them anymore.

Almost two years after we divorced, long after I had deleted most of my Instagram posts (and eventually archived the rest in an attempt to start over), I got a message from a stranger. She had spent years talking to a brick wall; messages from strangers go to another inbox, and so I sometimes don't see them for years before something one day gets my attention. There were previously unseen messages from her about my hometown, my outfits, my piercings, my new tattoos. It was parasocial, but it was polite. I didn't mind. But on this day, for some reason, she got my attention. "Just saw your ex on Tinder. Meant to take a screenshot but I swiped no before I could," she wrote, this woman, I'll call her Mandy, a complete stranger who wanted to give me a heads-up about nothing. "Anyways, you're a beautiful soul Scaachi!"

Were my ex-husband and I capable of being friends, I'd be able to send him Mandy's message, and we could laugh about it one more time. "What a freak!" he'd say, which would comfort me, because it was a reminder that it was him and me together, no one else. "I can't believe she thought it was appropriate to tell you this about me! What right do you have in knowing what I'm doing at all?"

"I know!" I'd say to the ghost of my ex-husband, who now only lives with me through stories. I still work hard to try to remember the best parts of him, to pepper in the good parts while I consider the worst ones. "It's my own fault. I don't have a right to you like this anymore, and she doesn't have this right to me. I told her too much."

My ex-husband would agree. "It's your own fault. You let them think they were in this life with us. Now I'm gone, and all you have are the secrets you could never keep to yourself."

⚡

A few months before my marriage ended, I went to a very bad party. I'm sorry I keep writing like this, separating everything into a before and an after, and I'm not sure when I'll stop feeling like that. It's as if a barrier formed in my life in my early thirties; everything before was naive and argumentative and ridiculous and everything after was painful and empty and honest. I'm waiting for another crack of lightning to strike and change things again; maybe next time I'll get something good. Like a gun!

My friend Janet, a thirty-foot-tall Long Island native who generally has a better time at all parties than I do, invited me to a party featuring New York City's media enfants terribles. Anyone in a creative field will tell you they have a love/hate relationship with these kinds of networking events: karaoke with your colleagues and their partners (who conveniently work at places you'd rather work), drinks in the park with the other non-white writers you know, potlucks with the other people in your intern pool. They're a necessary evil: How else will you jump to a new job, make friends, have sex, figure out who to avoid for the rest of your career? But the thing about necessary evils is that they're . . . evil.

Janet offered to be my social wingwoman: she whipped me away when the discourse dragged on too long, when people wanted to talk about my personal life (rocky) or my career (stalled). I love Janet, but I especially love her as a tentpole for security. You can find her in any crowd by simply listening for someone yelling at a volume never previously heard by human ears, usually about pasta. She doesn't mean to yell, it's just the way she's best understood. "OH I LOVE STROMBOLI," I heard her scream at the back of the bar as I slowly ambled toward her like a baby deer looking for her mother. "NOT ME ORDERING ANOTHER OLD-FASHIONED. I REALLY LIKE YOUR HAIR—IT'S GIVING EDITH PIAF BUT WITHOUT THE NAZIS." Soon, I would be safe, standing directly behind her, overshadowed by her height, no one bothering to talk to me because they'd mistake me for one of her legs, or maybe a very bushy, swarthy tail.

When I was younger and more nervous about whether I'd have a career at all, I went to these parties more frequently. Among the worst of them was an event in Toronto called Press Pass, hosted by a cabal of media losers whose names I never fully learned. The bar night happened once a month at a venue across the street from the worst McDonald's in the city, where we'd crunch together on a patio and drink our little IPAs. Before arriving, I'd fret over my outfit, wanting to telegraph that I was a serious writer who should be taken seriously, but not *too* seriously. A good chunk of the guest list were male journalists working at places like *The Globe and Mail*, the *National Post*, and the *Toronto Star*, big papers that made these men feel like they were big deals. They'd hover around the young women in attendance, their beady little eyes twitching around like they were looking for food after a famine. Their legs would slowly laze outward until our knees touched; their hands would linger on my back when they tried to squeeze around me. "You're funny," these men would say to me, as if I didn't know, as if that wasn't my one and only protection in the world.

I went to these parties looking for a fight, and I did the same when I went to the party in New York with Janet. A decade had passed and I was still chain-smoking outside (now smoking from my own pack and not bumming from a stranger, I had *evolved*). My feelings were the same: Did these people know me? Did I matter? Was I valuable? Were they keeping a mental list of my losses? Would I soon be just a morsel of gossip? Being a married woman offered me protection on the internet among these strangers: I was a *wife*. I was on a team that chose me and only me. I looked through the crowd—Janet near the bar, this time yelling about how PUGLIA IS SO GORGEOUS THIS TIME OF YEAR, YES, YOU ABSOLUTELY HAVE TO GO, REBECCA—and saw strangers with well-known Twitter avatars. No one knew each other at this bar, but they did in another place.

I took my drink to a corner and imagined what it would be like to tell these people the truth. An influencer I recognized from the internet flitted around the party, fresh off a host of allegations that she was a scam artist. She batted her blonde lashes at attendees while offering samples of a homemade serum. "This is giving me a rash," one woman hissed to

her friend after trying it on her cheek. A media reporter for
The Daily Beast was hunched over near the bathrooms, typ-
ing furiously on his phone, some tidbit that didn't matter,
which would end up in my feed in a few hours. Janet was
making new friends easily, reporting back with gossip about
how THAT DOOMED THROUPLE IS HERE AND THEY'RE
FIGHTING ALREADY. How would I explain my situation to
these people, if I had to? *I gambled and I lost. He didn't love
me the way I bragged that he did.* How would I explain Cait,
whose messages I was sitting on, and how she complicated
matters so much for me? I was exhausted from holding her
in as a secret, the same way you hold your breath. I needed
some air.

"ARE YOU HAVING FUN?" Janet asked me after finding
me tucked in a booth alone. She rested her hand on my
thigh, her martini half full and mine half empty. "WE CAN
GO IF YOU'RE NOT." Janet speaks in we: We can go, We
can stay, We can do whatever We want. But I was alone—
and I'd remain alone so long as I kept my ex-husband's
secrets, so long as I refused myself the truth. One day I
would tell her what was going on offline, the details I never
wrote in Instagram captions or in a newsletter. For now,
though, I didn't want to ruin her fun.

I squeezed her hand reassuringly. She got distracted by
another reporter, and loudly turned away to talk about THE
LAYOFFS AT BUZZFEED NEWS, YEAH, THEY'RE SO
DEPRESSING. I slid out of the booth, quietly. In front of the
bar, I checked my phone, my need for internet companionship still engaged despite my ongoing predicament: I had

a few mentions on Twitter, some likes on Instagram, and a message from the man who was, at that point, still my husband. "Are you coming home?" he asked, rhetorical. I mean, where else would I go?

When evil forces invade Parvati and Shiva's kingdom, Parvati's piousness is not necessarily her most helpful quality. Stand on hot coals if you wish, devote yourself to a soldier, or offer your full self to your partner—it's not what's needed of you anymore. Eventually, you have to fight for what you think is yours. Parvati transmutes into Durga in order to defeat a demon who takes the form of a buffalo, strong enough to defeat all the men who tried to face him. Durga is a more ferocious deity than Parvati; her several arms holding an array of weapons, but also a lotus flower, and an out-turned palm as if to welcome peace. She sits on a tiger or a lion, face beaming and rested. At her feet: coconut, pineapple, flowers. Durga is a fighter, but she's also the encapsulation of divine feminine energy—shakti. I hear Durga's chant in yoga classes taught by white people all the time, words I used to mouth along with my mother at the mandir without knowing what they meant. Om namah shakti shivaya.

My maternal grandmother's name is Durga. She lived and died in Jammu and Kashmir, spoke no English whatsoever, and we visited her sparingly. The few times I did get to see her, she held on to me for what felt like days, crying on my shoulder, her warm, round body shivering in grief. It made me uneasy to be the center of such loud feelings. I felt guilty about how I couldn't bring her into my life. Durga Maa is what they call her; the most terrifying warriors are, above all, mothers.

In New York, in my thirties, married and despondent, I didn't think the solution to my problems was motherhood. I couldn't imagine bringing another person into the troubles I was having with my husband; I didn't want our relationship to work only through the prism of the baby we needed to keep alive.

But as I left Janet at the media party, slipping out without anyone noticing, I considered that maybe the issue was too much Parvati and not enough Durga. I had been too passive. I was waiting for my devoutness to be recognized, to be rewarded. It wouldn't be, not because I hadn't tried, but because the prize would never be worth the self-evisceration. My feet were blistered, my shoulders aching from standing for a thousand years, waiting to be loved. My nani took care of my mother; she shepherded her into marriage, the only safe life she knew. My mother took care of me, and guided me into the same institution, believing as her mother did. Unlike them, I am still my own baby. No one takes care of me other than me. It's nice to think in the world of We, but when I turned my key in the lock of our apartment and entered a cold room, the fallacy of my marriage was starting to fade away. It was only ever just Me.

DHARMA

THE COSMOS
MAINTAINS HARMONY

"Get it? Got it? Good."

—SHAD, "THE FOOL PT. 1"

LOLITA, LATER

I was in a Target on West 34th Street the first time a man talked to me after I took my wedding ring off. I roamed the aisles after work, accumulating stuff for the apartment I was still a few weeks from moving into. I was staying at a friend's place in Park Slope, a neighborhood I didn't know well, full of happy families, children walking their very well-behaved dogs, couples holding hands. I hated my time there; I loitered in the city as much as possible. At least in midtown, *no one* is happy.

A man in a blue button-up shirt and matching blue eyes, wearing no jacket despite the cold, approached me with a wide smile. "Hi," he said, so collegial that I thought maybe he mistook me for a Target employee. I took stock of myself, wearing a thin layer of expired makeup that did nothing to hide the bags under my eyes, carrying an armful of strange but depressing home goods. I hadn't lived alone since I was eighteen, so I decided to pick up singles of everything: one mug, a single white plate, single pieces of cutlery all in different shapes and finishes ("I don't know what I like anymore," I whispered to the curves of a cereal spoon). I was building a life fit for loneliness, and here was some guy hitting on me in a Manhattan Target.

"Why don't you have a jacket on?" I asked him. "It's February."

"I work around the corner."

"So you just ducked into Target without your jacket?"

"Yeah."

"What are you shopping for?"

"Nothing."

"Then why did you come to Target?"

"Why did *you* come to Target?"

I held my treasures aloft. "To buy this one, lone, speckled bowl."

Jason seemed like a nice enough guy. He followed me through the aisles for a while, asking me questions and trying to get me to soften. He worked in finance and lived in New Jersey. He liked golf and craft beer. He had noticed me looking at pepper grinders and thought I was pretty and wanted to know my name.

It had been years since I had given a man my name, and I was still at the beginning of my split. Being hit on felt onerous, and I had developed a new, sticky kind of paranoia around men. Through my career, and through my marriage, I had worked on countless stories about terrible men: I wrote about men who raped their wives and girlfriends, who cheated their business partners, who lied under oath, who talked about teenage girls like they were sluts who got what they deserved. Every day, I heard from the world's most unreliable narrators, and tried to parse what was true, what was fair, and what was worth my time.

One particular week in junior high health class, the girls and boys were split into different rooms for two distinct presentations from an outside group. The organization was hired by the school every year to talk to each side about sex, puberty, and the horrifying incoming changes to our bodies (or, in many of our cases, the horrifying ongoing changes that struck us a little too early, like we were werewolves transforming at 4:30 p.m. when the sun and moon are both hanging in the sky). On the girls' side, a punky young woman with black micro-bangs and dark lipstick had us stand in a large circle, shoulder to shoulder with each other, popular girls mixed in with the rest of us plebs.

"I know it's hard to not think about what the boys are doing in the other room," she said from the center of the circle, "but I want us to focus on our own thing."

She walked around us, making eye contact with each of us, unsmiling and intense. "Today, we're going to work on showing someone who's bothering you that you're not someone to mess with." While she circled us, she had us glare back at her, giving her our most don't-fuck-with-me-fellas glare. She stood in front of us, scowling, directing us to scream "NO" and "GO AWAY" in her face as if to an imaginary male predator. I stifled laughter watching some of the girls take it, as I saw, *too seriously*: Skylar's face straining and beet red as she screamed "LEAVE ME ALONE," or A.J.'s eyes flashing with rage as she silently glowered at the instructor. When our hour was up, the instructor softened into a sweetheart again, congratulating us on finding our voices, and encouraging us to use them whenever we needed to.

She never said we were learning these particular skills of emotional self-defense against boys and men, but why else separate us by gender? Men were a breed perhaps worthy of fear, but certainly worthy of suspicion. This never squared away with the understanding of men I had formed at home: Men were like my father. They were helpless, sometimes unkind, but ultimately malleable. They didn't know where the can opener was. They needed us more than we needed them.

I wasn't allowed to date and it was always expected I'd come around to some kind of arranged union, so I dated in secret—revealing my relationship with my ex to my family was a significant rebellion, even if I was an adult when I committed it. But I also wasn't permitted male friends, or really any kind of significant male relationships. And so from an early age, boys and men could only fit in one of two categories: saviors and husbands, like in the movies, or villains and creeps, like the kind of guy you're trained to scream at—"HELP, THIS MAN IS FOLLOWING ME"—until he goes away.

Later, when the girls' side of the class reunited with the boys, we asked them what they learned while we worked on our defenses. "He drew a diagram of what it would look like if men had babies through their penises. Then we talked for a while about how gross that would be and so it's a good thing women are the ones who have to do it."

This is the childish archetype of man I returned to in my head as I reentered the world as a single woman. I hadn't been without a partner since I was twenty, and so baby-woman was indeed the right tone to strike. *Goo goo ga ga, I've never been on a dating app and I can't tell if I find you revolting or if I'm just afraid of you.*

My single friends were quietly excited for me to start dating, for us to cosplay *Sex and the City* over cosmos, wearing uncomfortable shoes, finding power in our solo status. It was a nice idea, but how could I trust a man again? Not even for marriage or a serious relationship—how do I let one of them in my house without worrying about him stealing all these nice, mismatched spoons I'm buying? How do I trust one with my body? How do I know they're not lying to me? Besides, why would anyone *want* to date me? Thirty-something and recently divorced is already a tough sell, made worse by the fact that I am pathologically determined to write about anyone who comes near me.

"I think I might spend a long time alone," I told my book editor over margaritas and Vogue Menthols on the beach. "No one will want to go out with me after they read anything I've ever written."

She laughed and lit a second cigarette from her first, looking out at the steadily setting sun. "Honey, I have some news for you: men don't read."

———

141

In the first grade, at Kingsland Elementary, a school that has since been decommissioned for what I trust were good reasons, we had an igloo-building competition every winter. Makes sense, a group of mostly white children building an igloo several kilometers away from Tsuut'ina Nation, while learning about Canada's Indigenous people in the past tense. Our parents would rinse out a two-liter carton of milk, fill it with water and food coloring, and freeze it overnight. In the morning, we'd trudge to school early with our icy cartons, rip them open in the playground, and start building igloos from our stained ice blocks. Teachers would pour water to help the blocks fuse, and we'd pat crunchy snow into the crevices. It was the only time grades one through three could work together, the bigger kids working on closing the top, while the little ones packed the bottom with stiff snow to keep the foundation strong. If you were lucky, you got to sit inside the igloo as the last brick was placed into the ceiling; you'd watch the sun get blocked out, filtered through blue and red and yellow milk carton blocks. Sit inside and you'd feel the cold settle into something liveable. You were alone in there, just the colors of the ice keeping you company, while you listened to the muffled sounds of kids running around outside the igloo, screaming, together, without you.

This is what I thought about, carrying my one bowl, my one plate, my one set of chopsticks. I thought about locking myself in an orb of ice, big enough for just me, where I could put in place that final brick. I could block out the sun. I could be alone, again, by design. Hadn't I earned it?

———

Jason followed me to the checkout. He asked for my number. When I told him I was just a few days out from my marriage, he beamed: "Me too!" he said. "We can be divorce buddies."

"You know what?" I said. "I don't know a lot of divorced people. Why not?" I took his number. And later, when I completed a public records search on him—as I eventually would do for every man who asked me out on a date for the following two years—I was smug to see my suspicions verified. "Does your wife know you're getting a divorce?" I texted Jason that night. "Did you tell her that you'd be divorcing when you remortgaged your house together three weeks ago? Should I call her? Would it be best to send her a text or an email at any of the following three email addresses connected to her name?"

While my phone filled with messages from Jason begging me not to tell her, not to call his wife at her job, not to tell his father-in-law who was also his boss, not to get him in trouble for the wretched acts of a pitiful man, I felt myself place that last brick of ice in my wall. I blocked out the sun. I would not let another man ruin my cold little home, built just for one.

⚡

Don't worry, I see it now. I get why people recoiled when I told them my husband's age and mine. I hear it. I heard it back then, too; I just didn't care. We met when I was twenty and he was thirty-three. It was obvious that my thoughts turned to our age gap when I turned thirty-three myself: I considered what it might be like to go out with a twenty-year-old. The thought is neither enticing nor illicitly titillating. It sounds like work.

But I liked being the younger wife. He was happy to leave a party early. We never drank without having a nice meal first. There was no need to walk the twenty-six minutes it would take to get to the movies; we could just take a cab. He had a little bit of money and a strong sense of self. He seemed to stand taller than me even though we were nearly the same height. He already knew everyone in Toronto, knew who to introduce me to, knew which fork to use at which restaurants. On our first date, he asked for my middle name and when I told him what it was—Lalita, named after my grandmother—he threw his head back in triumphant laughter. He asked for proof. "So you're basically a Lolita," he told me, shaking his head, looking at my ID, still thinking my middle name was a Nabokov reference. "A literal Lolita."

It did not matter that my middle name was not in fact Lolita, nor that I was far from a Nabokov nymphette. We carried that joke through our entire relationship, me as Lo and him as Humbert Humbert. I was his child bride. I was the light of his life, the fire of his loins, his sin, his soul. I never stopped the gag long enough to tell him that it was getting tired, that this joke in hindsight was starting to sour as I aged. By the time we got divorced, I hated the joke more than I hated him. For a decade, his name as a contact in my phone was "Hum." I'd sing a low warble of it into his ear when I'd come home from work trips, exhausted and thrilled to sink into his skin again: *Hummmmm.*

We could make this joke because we were sure to be the exception of a May/December relationship. We would stay together: There would be no ill-fated split where everyone rallied around me and said, "Well, we told you so." (This would, indeed, happen.) There would be no gaps in our understanding of each other, even though we were a full generation apart. (This, too, would happen, eventually at a near-daily clip.) And above all else, there would be no discrepancy of power, no innate belief that he was smarter than me or wiser than me or that I required babysitting or that he was slow and stodgy, or that one day he'd get bored of me, because I would get older, wouldn't I. (You know how the rule of threes works. I don't have to spoon-feed this to you, right?)

A key tenet of an age-gap relationship, namely in the courtship stage, is how older men underestimate younger women. This has been an ongoing narrative in my life, not just in my romantic relationships but sometimes in my friendships with men, in my day job as a reporter, in arguing with a customer service representative for an airline that canceled my flight and is claiming they don't owe me a free hotel stay in a city I already live in. (You better believe I'm going to make them put me up at JFK's Hyatt Regency. I don't even want it, but I'll make them do it out of sheer spite. The important thing is that *no one* wins.)

When acquaintances were surprised to hear of my divorce, they usually reacted in the same way: "You know, the only real red flag I ever saw was your age difference." It's an easy thing to point at, a behemoth thirteen years between us. No one would doubt me if I said we divorced because it was too challenging for one person to be in the tumult of her late twenties while the other is in the disarray of his early forties. People assume that my ex-husband underestimated me, like most older men do. They assume that I got older and he simply didn't like having to share control with someone steadily standing in her own power. They think he liked my age more than he liked me.

For a while, after we split, I believed this. I liked the kind of narrative it drew for me: *I was simply too much woman. He wanted a little girl and I was growing up. I fell into someone else's Lolita complex.* It was tidy. It made me feel good even when I felt awful. "I *told* you," my father once hissed to my mother when we talked about my divorce. He didn't even need to tell me what he was talking about; I knew he was referring to my ex's age, that he had told my mother it was unseemly and gross, that it would come back to haunt us. Our age gap was an easy issue to hang my sadness on; it made sense to me and to other people, and presented a neat narrative for me to tell myself. If I found someone my own age, all my problems would soon be solved.

This was what I thought about as I moved into my own apartment, as Janet ran smoke ripples of burning sage around my bed frame and mattress. "What's that for?" I asked her, holding a mint-green air fryer that I did not need, but had bought anyway. I was going to become the kind of person who air-fried things. (I used it twice.)

"IT'S SO THAT YOU GET RAILED," she said, wafting the bundle of twigs. "IT IS SO THAT YOU CAN FINALLY GET RAILED."

Sex was the preoccupation for my friends once I became single, but I was still running forensics on my dead marriage. Was it indeed our ages that made it impossible? Was I lacking the benefits of being with someone in my own generational bracket with my own reference points? Even bad news contains good information, and I could learn a lesson from this. Men my age have even more years to disappoint me. Why not be a Lolita forever?

⚡

I still can't believe how many people asked me, in the immediate months following my separation, whether I'd get married again. My parents barely waited four months before they told me not to allow this "life event" to "harden me to the possibilities" of a second husband.

"Is this the plan?" my dad asked me once. "To be single, forever?" There was a new family of Punjabis who had moved nearby; they had some sons, and perhaps I'd want to meet them. "What do you even want in a man?" he asked, before thinking too hard about the answer and burping from a sudden influx of stress-related GERD.

"What will you do if you don't remarry?" my mother asked me later, as if having a husband was the same as having a purpose, or at least a worthy preoccupation. Her questions to me were like asking someone who had just gotten their jaw wired shut whether they'd be interested in a juice cleanse in the near future. I was just trying to get over the first marriage, to rebuild myself as an independent, interesting, healthy person. I couldn't imagine a world where I shared a bathroom with someone again, where they'd hear me fart out aloo gobi for the third night in a row, where we'd floss together and let the horny romance die down into something more manageable, like when you walk through Target together, buying toilet paper and toothpaste and oh, look at this vase, do we need another vase?

I already suspected my lack of dating experience from the last decade of monogamy wasn't going to serve me well. For a while, I felt like some child of God raised in a restrictive religious sect that had married me off as soon as they could. When people learned how long I was shacked up, they talked to me like I had recently been defrosted in a cryogenic lab. "Who was the president when you went in?" they asked. "Have you heard of cell phones? Do you know about 9/11? Things are just so different now." With everyone I went out with, I had to perform a kind of normalcy to convince them that I was mentally well, and that if we had sex I wouldn't start crying about my ex-husband, that I wouldn't lay all my baggage at the feet of some stranger who just wanted to have a few cocktails in Bed-Stuy.

I was thankful for the abundance of apps that didn't even exist the last time I was single. They're awful, I know, I get it, I see why you were all complaining so much, but they also helped me cut down on small talk I wasn't ready to have. It was a great way to flip through a catalog of human meat:

six foot one, lean, 77 percent Colombian, gamey. Five foot seven, thick in the rump, pure Australian (and will tell you about it), salty. Five foot ten but pretending to be six feet tall, dense, tough but, ultimately, pliable. I wasn't sure if I would ever feel hungry enough to eat again, but it was nice to see what my options were. I always study the menu before I get to the restaurant.

As is customary when you get divorced, I went out with a lot of hot idiots. Just a parade of the most useless men in any of the city's several boroughs, all with the kind of shoulders that make you want to scale him like you're King Kong and he's the Empire State Building. No brains; just teeth so straight you want to play them like a xylophone. Arms the size of oil barrels. Pert butts, clear skin, take off your shoes at the door, please. I went out with a guy who ignored me the entire time to look at his own OnlyFans account on his phone. Another guy seemed to have never kissed a human person in his entire life, using mostly teeth, reminding me a bit of the dinosaurs in *The Land Before Time*. One pleaded with me to let him paint my toenails and then had the audacity to do a terrible job. One young man lectured me at a book launch about how he was a libertarian, which he explained by describing what was actually a textbook definition for socialism. I saw a fellow writer a handful of times who mostly wanted to talk about who *The New York Times* might tap to be their next media reporter after Ben Smith quit to start his own media company. (Truly, nothing drains your sexual battery quite like hearing the name of your former boss float through the conversation as you try to unlatch your own bra because your date lacks the basic dexterity.) One guy told me he'd vote for Joe Rogan for president if he could, only to amend his answer to Alex Jones when I gave him another chance to answer. An exceptionally attractive man (a non-white immigrant, no less!) lectured me on how ACAB was bullshit and then told me to "calm down" when I disagreed with him, so I popped my hot ass off that barstool and took a very depressing subway ride home alone. They varied in race and height and profession and state of mind, but they shared one thing: they were stupid.

I liked stupid, though. Stupid was good. It let me feel like I could escape these human interactions at any moment. It made me feel like I wasn't crushable, like I would never be crushed again. My ex-husband wasn't stupid, despite whatever other critiques I could lob at him. He was erudite and smart and wily. Being married to him was marrying into a chess game I didn't know we were playing. When I started dating again, I was trying to unfurl myself from the divorce, a process that would take far longer than I had initially hoped. Even now, I remain curled up—I still feel a bit like a caterpillar, crunched together, hiding from a predator. Expose your belly at the risk of being consumed.

⚡

The first man I started seeing with any regularity after my husband became my ex-husband was a six-foot-tall Danish bartender and amateur stand-up (*Jeeeeesus Christ*) who I had taken to simply calling "The Dane." He was the dumbest man

I had ever met, a genuine, bona fide, undisputed empty skull. Not a single thought rattled around in there. He was *Flowers for Algernon* in the first chapter with no promise of progression. He was also much older than me, older than even my ex-husband. The Dane seemed well aware of what a moron he was, and so he was never able to be condescending, he'd never even try. Unfortunately—or fortunately, depending on how highly you think of me—The Dane was my ideal male specimen for that moment in my life. His hair and eyes and skin looked like they were made of ice; he looked a little like a contemporary Guy Pearce, but mostly like a sexy Mr. Freeze if Mr. Freeze became a hot Nazi. (He wasn't a Nazi, to be clear. He was simply a burnout. Trust me when I say that I checked.) He had no body fat, abs so well-defined that they made me laugh when he took his shirt off, and he was covered in the most ill-conceived tattoos I have ever seen in my life. On one side of his neck, his estranged teenaged son's name. On the other side, the name of a dog he'd had, fifteen years earlier, now very much dead. He wore a heavy silver signet ring on his pinky, which seemed like the only possession of his that had any real value. All of his shorts looked like he'd attacked them with a rusty Swiss Army knife in 1988.

The Dane looked at me like I was digestible and I liked it. He liked the tattoo I have on my right arm of a sword diving into a heart that says "brat." Soon, he called me by that name exclusively. "I'll be seeing you, brat," he'd text me when he was leaving work. "Nice seeing you, brat," he'd text the day after. No longer a nymphette, I advanced to something with a rougher edge to it. I felt like dessert. He was terribly gentle;

most of our time together was spent lying around while he dragged the tips of his fingers along my arms and neck like he was making ASMR videos. He only asked vague questions; he seemed fine with my need for privacy. He knew what I did for work but not where I did it. He knew I was sad but not why. I called my friends to coo about The Dane. "He's perfect," I said. "He's the dumbest of them all."

My friends did not agree. "A Scandinavian kink?? How *boring,*" Adrian said. "He looks like a villain's understudy who gets killed three-quarters before the end of the movie. He's like a *Fight Club* extra. Did you really get out of that marriage just to waste your time with *this*?"

"Oh, come *on*. How old is he again?" Baby Braga asked when I told him about The Dane. "What do you even talk about? 'Sweetie, don't forget to take your second Viagra.'"

Braga took his glasses off and pinched the bridge of his nose. "This makes it very hard to root for you, Scaachi."

We all brainstormed what kind of music I could play during our time together. The Dane liked techno. Techno? It was like talking to someone who had landed here from a time machine originally set in Berlin in the nineties.

"There's a whole Billie Eilish between us," I said to him once, and based on his reaction, I felt very strongly that he did not know what a Billie Eilish is. Everyone in my life was tired of my old-man fetish, as it had been codified in my friend group, my propensity for men so much my senior that when we walked around in public, people would look, and squint, clearly wondering, *Green card marriage? Or maybe he is simply infirm, and she's his helpful Dominican nurse.*

———

Most people read *Lolita* wrong. Initially, I read it as a treatise on why men need to keep their wits about them among young temptresses: I was around thirteen when I picked it up, and then saw the Jeremy Irons movie soon thereafter. I was too young to know the difference between playing like you had power and actually having it. When I was in my twenties, I read it again, this time seeing Dolores clearly: she was a little girl whose stepfather wanted to fuck her, who took her away from her mother (who was also of little use), who raped her while they were on the road together, who gave her no choice but to run to another much older man because it was the only protection she'd ever known. These were the only two versions of Lolita I understood, as if there could be no other interpretations.

Was *that* what I was doing? In reality, my ex-husband was not the first older man I had gone out with. They were in their late thirties and early forties when I was nineteen. They were established journalists who had no business fucking around with a new employee, investment bankers, a professional race car driver, a barista who once got mad at me when I called him for help because someone was following me home from a bar. They all had crow's feet, which I liked.

Adrian implored me to date someone my own age, but I had no interest. Dating older felt natural; I was raised with brothers and cousins all a decade-plus my senior, and I didn't think I knew what to do with a man closer to my age. The Dane was safe. I knew what to do with a man that close to death. I knew what kind of ego-stroking they required (ask if they can open a jar of peaches for you), I was already briefed on the music that Gen X men wanted to tell me about (wow, I have never heard of The National, tell me more, do they play guitars?), and I have read plenty of David Foster Wallace so I'm familiar with their self-made mythos (men would rather read *Consider the Lobster* annually than go to therapy once).

My ex-husband and I used to laugh about the prosaic literary tastes of straight, white men. In some other timeline, we're reading Blake Butler and debating the merits of his sentence structure. In this one, however, I point men of a certain age toward my bookshelf, like a sexy grim reaper, guiding them toward the light between my legs. "I didn't know Jon Stewart wrote a short story collection," these men say, tenderly tipping the cover open to see the table of contents. I fold down the corner of my bedsheets.

I never liked men my age. My father fostered a firm distrust of boys, including my peers. When he drove over to pick me up from my high school one afternoon, he caught me sharing a bag of candy with a male classmate.

"That's how you get disease," he said when I got in the car. "Hand-to-hoof-to-mouth disease. You get it from sharing candy. Don't look it up, just trust me."

But only after Jeff assaulted me did I start to fear men my age. It was later that I felt more aware of how small they made me feel, how fast they moved, how rarely they made eye contact with me. Men my age knew my friends and my colleagues and could spread rumors about what they took from me, claiming I gave it up freely. I spent years afraid of what Jeff would do with the information he had about my body. His youth, I worried, would add to his credibility and take away from mine. Even if that data was taken from me by force, calling me a "slut" in public still felt like it had the ability to ruin my life and end my career before it started. With older men, I felt more in control. I had some leverage— real or perceived, it didn't matter—because my age was so deliciously inappropriate. They were afraid of me; afraid of what their friends would say about the age gap, afraid of seeming lecherous at work if it got out that they were court- ing an intern. Older men had fewer hang-ups about my sex- ual proclivities, how many partners I'd had, what *kind* of slut I was. I liked feeling like I had something to bring to the table. They could pretend I was innocent and usable, and I could pretend they were capable of protecting me. I could live like every older man out there was my father: ultimately, a harmless, friendly guy who just wants to take a nap.

No one believes me when I tell them that I had power in all my relationships *because* of how much younger I was. I get it: it sounds like I'm trying to save face from what was clearly a poor decision. But it's true that being younger afforded me more in my marriage than I would have gotten were we the same age. I always had something he wanted: thirteen fewer years alive.

I have spent so much of my own life trying to assess whether I have any power or not. I never get closer to an answer. I ensnare an older man into falling in love with me and then he takes excellent care of little old me: I have power. *Roe v. Wade* becomes a piece of history I'll tell my niece about one day: I have no power. My partners were always nervous about our age difference: I have power. I grew up but they didn't, leaving me rug-burned and isolated: I have no power. They live in an infantile fixation and are worse off for it: I have power. I'm at the county clerk's office alone filing for divorce from someone born in the late seventies, and the older woman helping me flinches when she sees our distinct decades of birth: no power at all.

I seek power everywhere because I feel like someone is always trying to take it from me. And because I ascribed so much power to being the Lolita, it meant that the power dissolved as soon as our marriage did. If there was power in being the young wife, then there's nothing left for you when he moves on. The women my ex dated after me were all his own age, something that relieved me (he's not a predator, he just didn't like me very much, is all) and infuriated me (so, what, I've soured you on all younger women now?). No wonder I looked for older men to tell me I was still a Lolita. Tell me my skin is so smooth. Admire how the lines on my face haven't yet set into something more permanent. Recount your evening prescription medication routine so we can laugh about how long it is, and how I don't fear death at all.

I never let The Dane get too close to me. He asked to sleep over—perhaps because, as I suspected, he did not own a bed anywhere—but I always cheerfully said no and sent him home with an ice-cold Diet Coke and a blown kiss. A few times he asked if I had any spare copies of my first book lying around. "Nope," I said, casually glancing at my closet door, which housed hundreds of copies. I just didn't want him in my brain. I didn't want him to get to know me. I didn't want him to read anything I had written; even sending him a text felt too intimate, never mind showing him a host of love stories about another man who now hated me.

What was he going to do with my book, anyway? I remained unconvinced he could read.

No one knows what happens to Lolita when she grows up. In the book and in the movies, Lolita dies before she reaches adulthood, while she's in childbirth herself. We never know how she felt about Humbert Humbert, her stepfather, because she never gets the benefit of age and hindsight. We never know what she thought about Clare Quilty, the man she eventually runs off with, because she's never old enough to be trusted with her own feelings. Lolita is only ever viewed through a male author, and through the men who grew obsessed with her. That's for good reason, if you're the author: to give her a voice is to run the risk of viewing her as a victim, a survivor, a girl who's now a woman. In *Lolita*, Humbert Humbert predicts that "Dolly Schiller will probably survive me by many years," but of course she didn't, and she couldn't. No one wants Lolita to grow up. She'd have too much to say.

⚡

For some people, it's easy to find cruelty in a breakup. I don't know if my ex found it easy to be mean to me, but I remember every unkind thing he said as I was leaving.

"Do you think someone's going to put the work into you that I have?" he said to me in one of our last conversations. He told me how impossible it would be for another man to fall in love with me, how they'd grow exhausted by the labor required to get close to me.

"I don't think I need that much work," I said, silently cataloguing all the ways I was impossible.

He was bringing a glass to his lips when I replied, a statement apparently so absurd he stopped short and brought the glass back down to the counter with a contemptuous *thud*. "Yeah, baby. You do. You need a lot of work." Here: I was baby-woman one final time.

I was used to hearing this—everyone in my life has, at some point, told me that I am a *lot*. The Koul women are notorious for how they can drain a man's energy. Do you have someone in your life who you want to wear down like the raw nubbin of a leftover eraser? We can do that. *I* can do that. It's one of our dominant genes, the way we all have dark hair that curls in the same pattern at our foreheads, or how our foreheads are, to begin with, only two inches tall and yet seven inches wide.

But it hurt when my ex said it because I believed it to be true. I didn't think that I'd find anyone who would want to put up with me again. I believed that I was overwhelming, a lot to manage, and that I *needed* management. I didn't know how to be alone. I required a personal boss. Maybe my marriage would have fared better had I noticed that I'd let my husband become my babysitter. Maybe it would've given us even a few more good years.

More than anything else, I took my ex seriously. He was a serious person, a businessman, someone who wore a suit every day. He woke up earlier than me, which made him an adult. Our dynamic *was* a May/December one, but not necessarily because of our ages. Early on, we quietly agreed that he was the grown-up. My name was never on a lease. I didn't set up our gas bill. Our cell phones were on a family plan which he paid for the both of us. The internet account was in his name. He knew how to fix the loose knob on our stove. He set up my banking and investments to his taste—I had none, since I still believe that if they really wanted to, they could just print more money. (Who's *they* here? You know. *They*!) In all my time with him, I had just been pantomiming adulthood. I don't know if he liked being the grown-up in the room or if he just accepted his fate based on my own inertia. But I was never an adult. I was never an equal partner.

When it was clear our marriage would not survive, I asked my husband how he wanted to become my ex-husband. "Do you want to file the papers or should I?" Days before, he said he was going to file, but as he hardened and softened at the same time, he decided that if I wanted the divorce, I'd have to file the papers myself. This, I knew, was not his style, and so it felt like a kind of punishment. This was a grown-up's task, the kind of work that my ex would have done were he still my husband: tracking down paperwork, getting signatures, standing in line at the county clerk's office, charming a woman named Denise so she'll expedite the filing, just for you, just for those baby blues. (I never charm anyone like this, seeing as my eyes are black.) Even though the divorce was my idea, I still thought he would handle it like the December usually does. Even though I asked for the divorce, I still felt like it was his fault, like we were only splitting up because of him, and yet I was tasked with the labor of finalizing it. But my ex did exactly what I was always asking him to do: give me the reins, let me be the adult, let me handle it, trust that I am capable beyond my years. He finally did, but he did it at the very end, when it could only hurt.

If I wanted the divorce, I'd have to get it myself. And so I took a sunny fall Friday off from work to walk the four-hour round trip to the clerk's office, exactly $210 in hand, my documentation signed and stacked and notarized. I got the paperwork wrong twice before I got it right.

*

Lolita and Humbert Humbert are both white. When I read *Lolita*, I only paid attention to their age differences; I never considered the ways the story didn't apply to me. There was something inherently different about our marriage, not because we were immune to the issues that come with a May/December dynamic, but because one of us wasn't a part of the ruling racial class anywhere we ended up living. Strangers assumed it had been tough to tell my parents that I wanted to marry my ex-husband because he was white; I reassured them that my parents' issues were with our age difference. Age was so significant that I never had time to think about how his whiteness, and my lack thereof, was affecting us.

When Trump was elected, my ex-husband almost got in a fight at a party we were attending. Another journalist had sneered at how upset we all were, we the liberal snowflakes who couldn't imagine a world where a game show host accused of sexual assault could become president. I saw my then-boyfriend's knuckles go white as the skin tightened around his fist, and I knew we'd have to leave. I had seen the election results coming, and had told him for months that he should steel himself for what I knew was inevitable. He didn't believe me. In fact, there were many things he didn't believe me about: he stayed friends with white men I told him were abusing their power at work, some of our greatest arguments were about the ways capitalism could benefit him and not me (even as our incomes started to balance out), and he lived his life with an expectancy of expedited service that I just never had. Air Canada always seemed to offer him refunds. People called him "sir" wherever we went: "How come you never call me sir?" he said to me once, joking innocently, but it bothered me anyway. Did he really need another person to defer authority to him just because he's a white guy in a suit?

Sometimes I admired how he went through life—barreling, impolite if he needed to be, fearless at night going down streets that I asked that we perhaps avoid. Other times, I resented it; he didn't listen to me until it was abundantly clear he had to. My ex-husband had good politics, but only after I convinced him of it.

"You think everything is racist," he said, chuckling to

himself, after I told him that a news anchor on Canada's largest network had insulted me in a private phone call. "Some people are just foolish. It doesn't mean everything is about race."

Five years later, she was fired for saying the n-word in a meeting. "You were right," he told me. But I knew that. I already knew that. What I couldn't understand is why he'd never take my word for it, and why we always had to wait for more proof of what I had been saying all along.

Once I shook off The Dane—which I only did when I found out about his amateur stand-up career, wherein he stole two jokes from me for his own set—I vowed to stop dating white men. I hadn't gone out with a man of color since I was a teenager, a choice that never felt intentional to me but had its own consequences anyway. Would I have felt such urgency to tell my parents about my new, old boyfriend had he been South Asian? In my imagination, an ethnic version of my ex-husband would be more understanding of the complications of having Indian parents. I wouldn't have to explain my aversion to most beef and pork products, I wouldn't have to eat around his high-protein needs. Had I married a brown person, I wouldn't have to explain anything at all. Our house would be made of daal.

I built a fantasy of needlessness for me to live in. I liked the small, alone life I had built. I was still suspicious. If a man asked me out, my answer came out loud and distrustful: "Why? Are you trying to harvest my kidney?" But more irksome was the steady creep of loneliness, the way my body would sway if I smelled someone delicious on a subway car, bringing up the memory I was trying to suppress: that once, I woke up next to someone, every morning. I wanted to get close to someone without them getting too close to me. Being alone is lovely but, periodically, you need someone to like you enough that they want to taste the inside of your mouth.

I dreamed about being alone and needing no one, but if I had to imagine being with a man, I thought of more needlessness. I wouldn't *need* to justify my hot emotions to a man of color; he grew up with women like me and would get it, intrinsically. I wouldn't *need* to explain that he had to remain a secret from my family; he would understand the double life we all lead. I wouldn't *need* to ask him to celebrate Shivaratri with me instead of Easter; he could do it all, without an ask, without a request, without the burden of my stated needs. I winnowed my search to someone who needed nothing, just like me.

"I'm seeing a young man in Brooklyn," I told Adrian one afternoon. Adrian and I have never finished a conversation; one just bleeds into the next one and the one after that and the one after that. We were picking up wherever we'd left off, as usual.

He looked at me, pained. "What do you mean *young man*?" he asked. "Are you being ironic? Is he a septuagenarian? Does he have any of his original teeth?"

For a while now, Adrian and I have been calling each other our Twin Flame. It's not romantic; it's far uglier. The bad luck in our lives has always come in pairs. Our respective breakups happened around the same time, our parents had health scares around the same time, and when one loses a job, the other is soon to follow. He does not like it when I give him any news about my personal life, because his is soon to shift, too, a chain reaction further proving that our tether is out of our control. "If this one's also wearing ripped-up Ramones T-shirts and stealing your B material for his open mic nights, I don't want to hear about it," he said.

Adrian would warn me against going on too many dates with the wrong person: "You could lose a lot of time here." He said it like I was liable to sink, as if mediocre men on dating apps were quicksand. But Twin Flames would know; he was busy losing time with some woman he met at the zoo, and just wanted to spare me the same fate. (Adrian would, here, correct me with, "I didn't meet her *at* the zoo, we went *to* the zoo on a date! You're making her sound like she's one of the animals!" But this is my book, not Adrian's, and so: he was dating a large, flightless bird at the zoo, one of the emus with horrifying little red eyes, his pockets presumably filled to the brim with food pellets and proteinaceous crickets to keep her engaged.)

I had decided to play with someone my own age for once, and so I found him. He was in his mid-thirties, lived in Brooklyn not far from me, and was a personal trainer who looked like a personal trainer. He was neither the heady intellectual that my ex-husband liked to view himself as, nor the rambunctious adult baby that The Dane was. He called me *love*, which I hated, but I liked how his voice sounded like a hot toddy when he said it. He worked at a gym near my apartment, but he was never *my* trainer. I couldn't imagine having sex with someone who'd also watch me grunt my way through Bulgarian split squats. But what he was, above all, was age appropriate.

"He's just thirty-seven?" Adrian asked with the trepidation of someone being invited to a party where the theme is beating up people named Adrian. "Do you mean, like, in dog years?"

It sounds snide to say that The Trainer was diametrically opposed to my ex-husband in so many ways, but it felt impossible to not notice it. The Trainer was the first man I had dated in my generational bracket since before I was married. My ex was almost my height, white, comfortable in a conference room, and he believed Ben Stiller was the good guy in *Reality Bites*. The Trainer was tall, Caribbean, built like a tight end, and a little afraid of me; he spoke rarely, and when he did, he said everything slow and low and simmering, like a Crock-Pot telling you a secret. I had compared The Dane with my ex, too, but they had so much in common that the game stopped being interesting after the first few minutes.

I was still in my most cynical era when I met The Trainer, still unwilling to give anyone my first name. Anyone who came near me would first have to pass through a credit check, a public records search, a quick dig into their criminal record to see if they had any formal complaints lodged against them by women. If I had time, I'd check his dormant Twitter accounts to make sure he didn't used to be one of those guys who replied to everything Nicki Minaj posted with, "queen, please give me a chance."

This information highway did not go both ways: I've always left a bigger internet footprint than anyone I've met, and my first name easily leads to every piece of data that's ever existed about me. I didn't want to be googled before a date, to be gawked at through my work or the Instagram account I suppose I could privatize but I simply haven't, like the Tinker Bell that I am. My name is so uncommon, despite my pleas for people to start naming their most unbearable children after me, that I've never been able to hide. When The Trainer asked me for my name, I told him the first thing I thought of: "It's Lali," I said, truncating my La/Lolita title into a new cognomen. I was right to protect myself: in the background checks I ran on various men, I found stalking charges, unmentioned wives, civil litigation, false addresses, lies about their ages. One man's background check came back with formatting issues, which turned out to be because he'd had his record expunged in his early twenties. "I didn't set out to stab him," Brad told me. "It was self-defense." (When I told Adrian this, he just started groaning like he needed to be rebooted.)

"You registered as a Republican?" I asked one man over text, who had picked me up on the subway in FiDi, like only a probable white-collar criminal would. Minutes after he gave me his number, I looked up his name among New Jersey's voter rolls. I could tell he didn't live in lower Manhattan; he wore rimless reading glasses and had no tattoos.

"Yo, I don't even care about politics that much haha," he replied.

"So you REGISTERED as a REPUBLICAN?"

All The Trainer knew about me, for months, was that I was a writer. "I'm eager to read what you write about me," he told me once. "Though it would probably mean we no longer know one another. So, not that eager." Could *he* read? I never asked and was a little too spooked about the answer to try and find out.

In bigger ways, I liked having The Trainer in my life because he reminded me I had done a full rotation. We were only ever in a deep kind of lust. I thought about him all the time; The Trainer replaced my ex in my mind completely. We were not a couple, and there was no chance of that—indeed, we'd talk about how unlikely it was that we would ever get along in what we kept referring to as "the real world." The Trainer and I only saw each other in the confines of my apartment, play-acting at intimacy. We didn't go to dinner, we never met each other's friends, we didn't even broach the topic of going outside. We dated other people—or, I think we did, that was another thing we never discussed—and then collided back into each other every three to seven weeks. But seeing him was essential. It felt restorative, even if it was flimsy.

And indeed, we had a shorthand I never had with my ex-husband, which would never have been available to us even if our marriage had been functional. When I complained about white people, The Trainer laughed and squeezed my leg. There was no discussion about how, actually, neo-liberalism has a place in a functional democracy. When my mother got sick, and I had to leave town for a month, I didn't have to talk him into why it was a good idea for me to go. "It's your mom," he said. "What else is there to do but go home?" He texted me every few days, asking about aunty. I wish I had better language to explain the ease with which everything came, purely because our backgrounds had commonalities. Is there a word, in Kashmiri or Hindi or anything else, that describes the immediate comfort of spending time among a community similar to yours? I spent night after night with The Trainer, sometimes feeling like I was being unfaithful to the white husband I no longer had, who I'd once loved and protected and defended for so long. It felt disloyal to admit the truth: his whiteness was something we had to overcome, though I suspect he always thought it was my race that created the bulk of our burdens.

The Trainer was in my igloo. I let him in without realizing it. I don't remember making it big enough for two, but The Trainer rubbed my feet while we watched *Seinfeld* in there. We never made it to the episode that spoke to his role in my life the most: "The Stall." Puckish Elaine is dating a rock-climbing cool-guy who wears his baseball caps backward (big move for a white guy in the nineties, after all), whose best, maybe only asset is his beautiful face. When Jerry and Elaine talk about her new boyfriend, I could hear Adrian and me trapped in the same discourse about the same kind of guy. Adrian/Jerry calls him a "pretty boy," popping his collar to mimic the mimbo Elaine/I have grown so fond of.

"Jerry," Elaine said (or maybe I said it?), "I would be going out with him no matter what he looked like."

"Of course you would," Adrian said to me. "Of course you would," Jerry told Elaine.

It's painful to get what you want. It reminds you of when you didn't get anything at all. When The Trainer was kind to me, it made my stomach flip, like when you're left suspended in the air for a moment on a roller coaster. His sweetness made me nervous, like there was medicine coming in behind it, like he was tricking me. Feeling how much more comfortable I was with a person of color made my memories of my ex-husband shrivel up even more; it cast everything in new doubts and new unhappinesses. The Trainer lit incense in my apartment; bergamot, myrrh. He smelled like a familiar memory that I could never place; the smell of someplace you had been before. He brought bottles of wine and tightly rolled joints; he took his shoes off at the door without my asking. He'd run his fingers up and down my shins, an act so tender that it made me want to double over and retch. The gentler he was with me, the meaner I was, but he reacted the way a giant might when a scared townsperson throws a rock at his ankle, laughing and swooping me up with a veiny forearm. I had only been divorced for a few months when we met, but it had been several years since someone had been tender with me.

"Nice outfit," I said, sneering when he came over in his work clothes: tapered windbreaker, sweatpants, and a camouflage trucker hat. Ridiculous. Black Larry the Cable Guy, in my kitchen.

"Thanks!" he said, cheerfully, fully unaware that I thought he was dressed like a Patagonia Republican. He placed a bottle of red wine on the counter before greeting my (embarrassingly boy-crazy) cat with some scratches behind her ears. "This is my favorite hat." The Trainer shook his long hair out from under his cap, filled my space with his big body, and, even better, refused to notice when I was being a fucking bitch.

After six months of the most casual form of dating—no titles, no requirements, no demands—I told him my real name. I told him about Scaachi, about Lalita. I told him about literature's Lolita, about my own history as a pitiable Lolita avatar. I told him about my namesakes, all of them, about the way my ex-husband said my name, always a little wrong, always beyond repair. I told him how long it had been since I had dated someone my own age, and finally, someone who wasn't white. He kissed me on the forehead, again too tender for what we were careening toward. "Scaaaaah-chi," he said, learning the new contours of this name, smiling with his eyes still closed. "Scaaaaaah-chi." I pressed my fingers against his lips to feel my own name; I liked the way he said it.

⚡

I derive very little pleasure from dating, but I do like telling men I'm divorced to watch them react like I'm letting them know my vagina is full of teeth. Carlos, an electrician in yet another backward baseball cap who got too stoned to stay awake during our date, was taken aback. "You're divorced?" he said, holding my hand with the same tentativeness you might employ on an elderly woman in your neighborhood whose bones keep turning into sawdust. "But . . . you're so beautiful." Marc Anthony—his real name, based on the thorough public records search I did to find out if he was lying about this perfectly ridiculous name—bulged his eyes out so far that I distantly heard a *bo-yo-yoing* as his optic nerves dangled his eyes out of their sockets. "Shorty, how'd you get married and divorced *already*? I'm just getting started out here!"

Men often want to hear about the ways my marriage was awful. They want to suss out if I think it's my fault, or my ex-husband's. They're trying to gauge if I might be liable to get divorced more than once. Could they be next? Otherwise, it seems most likely that they just want to swoop in and be the savior: Some of them, you can tell, are just *itching* to be told that I haven't been able to have an orgasm since the split. They want to be the first. They want to restore my faith in men after a single fifteen-minute romp. The devastation that crosses their faces when I remind them that I have never needed a man for that is so exquisite, Neiman Marcus should bottle it as an Eau de l'Humiliation.

The Trainer never asked me about my divorce and, for a while, I loved him for it. With him, my life had just started: there was no Before The Trainer, there was only The Now, Together. My ex had been preoccupied with the details of my life when we were together, invested in what I did at work and if my diet affected my mood and how much I contrib-uted to my 401(k) and if I came home late and who my friends were and when I'd be visiting my parents in Calgary that year. At his best and worst, he was my proprietor.

But The Trainer offered me no management at all. Sometimes he had a solution to a small problem—"The slats under your bed need to be screwed down so they stop moving"—but unlike my ex, he wasn't proactive, he had no drive to be right. For a while, I admired this: I was so used to people showing me their most competitive sides through high executive functioning.

The slats under my bed still move. The Trainer never fixed anything.

✦

After my divorce, a trend went viral on TikTok where young women asked each other if they'd rather be stuck in the woods with an unknown man, or a bear. No details are known about the bear or the man, whether they've ever attacked anyone in the woods before, whether they're friendly beasts or not. Men on the app were incensed by the overwhelming consensus coming from women: we'd all feel much safer with the bear.

In 1976, Toronto-based author Marian Engel published *Bear*, a novella about a lonely librarian who falls in love with a wild bear. If you're wondering if she ends up fucking the bear, she absolutely does. "He licked. He probed. She might have been a flea he was searching for. He licked her nipples stiff and scoured her navel," Engel wrote. "When she came, she whimpered, and the bear licked away her tears." Sex is all she and the bear do, so much so that it becomes unsatisfying for her, the way he tears at her, but never with real interest. Why would he? He's a fucking bear. "Sometimes the bear half-ripped her skin with his efficient tongue, sometimes he became distracted. She has to cajole and persuade him. She put honey on herself and whispered to him, but once the honey was gone he wandered off, farting and too soon satisfied," Engel wrote. "'Eat me, bear,' she pleaded, but he turned his head wearily to her and fell asleep."

The librarian wanted to be consumed. She wanted to be wanted. She had, for so long, mistaken the harms the bear caused her to be tantamount to love, to sex, to meaningful passion. But the bear seems to hardly notice her at all. The problem of *Bear* isn't that the protagonist is having sex with a bear, it's that the bear just doesn't like her that much. She's the only woman living in the house in the woods, already alone and already desperate for affection. The book is called *Bear* for a reason: no one cares about the woman who's lonely enough to fuck the bear.

How many times could I prostrate myself at the feet of someone whose indifference I had confused for affection? The answer for a long time, it turned out, was just a little bit more, just a few more times, just one more night with him and then I'd be cured for sure. While my ex's cruelty felt more direct, like he was capable of clearly and concisely telling me how I was failing in our marriage, The Trainer's brutishness was obfuscated by his kind eyes, our low-pressure situationship, and the fact that I never really asked him for anything. My ex-husband's unkindness was a rock, something burdensome that I could get used to—you can get strong enough to carry anything around. But The Trainer's insensitivity was electric, like volts traveling from the soles of my feet to my crown. I didn't know how to get better at being electrocuted. He didn't even know he was doing it, so gentle was he at letting me down. It was a weaponized carelessness I had yet to experience. Men older than him did it differently; they were mean with intention and purpose. White men did it with the weight of dropping a hammer. He was so delicate in how he hurt me. The Trainer was a bear looking for food, indifferent to the source, and I couldn't stop feeding him.

I was, frankly, reassured to see that a man of color would be a disappointment, too. It made me feel better to know that my ex-husband's ultimate failing wasn't his age or his race, not really: he was just a man, like all the rest! When I asked The Trainer if he wanted to go to the park one afternoon, he balked as if I had gotten down on one knee. Our many months of hand-holding, of him wrapping a hand around my waist with pleasing pressure, of him texting me "how's your mom doing?" seemed to mean far less to him than it did to me. How cliche of both of us. He made me feel like such a *girl*.

He told me he liked me, sure, but he just wanted to be friends. He said it minutes after making my knees buckle, yet again. "Maybe this is something I have to work out in therapy," he said. I would have loved to be a fly on that wall, during his first therapy session, explaining the inciting event that led him to some guided introspection: "Well, I was texting her every day but then she asked to sit under a tree in Prospect Park and that just felt like too much, too soon. My mother, you say? Why do you ask about my relationship with my mother?"

The Trainer and I mellowed out into something wholly unsatisfying. More and more, he felt like my tennis doubles partner. He was just a guy I danced with. We were hobbyists.

"You've never even seen me in a jacket," I told him once, hoping it might nudge us into the world. There was something about the mundanity of a relationship that I missed: reading in the park, peeling a potato while he cuts an onion, squabbling about if it's pronounced charade (American English) or *charade* (Canadian English). I just needed more light.

I forgave him little trespasses for months, eventually for an entire year. I was so used to forgiving men, I came by it easily, especially since The Trainer's failures were so minuscule compared with my ex-husband's. So what if he never wanted to leave the house with me? If he seemed a little embarrassed by the idea of being seen with me in public? If he didn't know my birthday or my favorite movie, never met anyone I ever loved, or even saw me eat? *How boring*, I thought, *to have fallen into the same trap of a barely there man*. I had built this house just for me; he ruined it by reminding me that I still wanted to make room for someone else, no matter how little room was left. I resented that I still had the muscle memory to make space for someone who made none for me. I thought it was okay because he was my age. Somehow, we were equals, even though he kept a polite distance from me always, and I was so swept up in him that I wanted to drink his blood through a curly straw.

"Do you realize you've never seen me in shoes?" I told The Trainer, trying the angle again, one of the last times I saw him. "Or socks. Or jeans. You've never seen me walk more than fifty steps in a row. You've never seen me walk down a flight of steps. You don't know what my brother's name is. You've never asked me if I'm allergic to kiwi! You don't know how much I spend a month on fresh pomegranate! You don't even know what my favorite natural disaster is!"

"*Are* you allergic to kiwi?" he asked. I am, but I didn't know why I bothered to tell him. He would never remember, and he would never need to.

⚡

I'm alone again, but I try to remember that I've always been alone. I was alone with my ex-husband; he had checked out of the relationship as soon as he brought a white woman into it. I was alone with The Dane, his brain too weak and brittle to handle a conversation with me. I was alone with The Trainer, a bear who was looking for honey. None of them kept me company. I was alone this whole time with none of the fringe benefits of one's own bed or eating Zingy Zaps for dinner or not having to listen to a man talk about his weight-lifting schedule at the local Retro Fitness. I'm trying to remember that it's a privilege to be alone. Dolly Schiller never really grew up, but she was also never really alone either; she went from her mother to Humbert Humbert to Clare Quilty to her husband, and then to death. No one involved in her story, not even her author, left her to her own devices.

Nothing is permanent, not even me. The trouble with my marriage, ultimately, wasn't really his age or his race. It was always easier to blame the things I could see on his face or on his birth certificate, than the unbearable truth: one day, he just didn't love me as much as I hoped.

I'm lonely, sometimes, but I'm lucky enough to have built this home for one, this cold hub. Like most women, I'm conditioned to think that a man will come and save me from the life I made on my own. But I know he's not coming because he doesn't exist. I'll remember that it's been weeks or months since someone touched me, but it's also been years since someone told me what to do. I'm lucky to get to trust myself. I wonder what it'll be like to invite someone in—to move the green chair so it's next to the wall to make room for their little table, to replace some of my books with theirs, to have to house a copy of *Lolita*, years after I left my original with my very own Humbert Humbert.

I am lonely because I have grown up. The light in my apartment filters in through my curtains, spilling pink and green and blue sunbeams in my space. I'm alone in here, but I feel like a kid again, gazing at ice blocks dyed to make the cold beautiful, for however long it lasts.

AUSPICIOUS

⚡

My mother wanted me to get married and I thought it would be selfish of me to not give her this one little thing she asked for.

In the fifth grade, when I cut off all my hair, she kept it in a Ziploc bag in the big freezer in the garage. (Are you an immigrant family if you don't have a "big freezer" in another part of the house, filled with two-month-old meat, frozen tubs of rajma in old Becel containers, parathas, and emergency cheese pizzas for when your mother has to go to an aunty's house and you're home alone to fend for yourself?) I had my hair shaped into a cursed pixie cut that made me look like Moe Howard in the body of a sluggish twelve-year-old. "This is for your wedding day," my mother told me proudly, writing my name on the bag of hair as if she'd discover it one day and wonder, *Well,* whose *hair is this?* Her plan was to turn the hair into extensions when I got married. "Much cheaper," she said, nodding.

Twenty years later, when I called my parents to tell them I was getting a divorce, I couldn't get the words out. They answered my video call and I already appeared flushed from crying. I had no plan for how to tell them, and was quietly hoping to perhaps die, immediately, in my chair, to avoid the burden of saying the words.

"What's wrong, beta?" Papa asked me, a tenderness in his voice I had never heard before, which only made me cry more because I knew I was entering unknown territory with him. He had never been so soft or so concerned. I had never seen his face in distress without seeing a slash of anger under the surface. "What's wrong? Why won't you tell me what's wrong?"

My father isn't perceptive. He would never be able to guess. But my mother was in another room, had not yet seen my face, and had yet to hear me say a word. I could hear her put the top of the pressure cooker on, sealing it so it would start screaming in twenty minutes. Still, she knew: "Are they separating?" she asked. Papa looked back at me, puzzled, and all I could do was crumple into my hands. "Oh, no," he said, softly, and I had visions of hundreds of my strands of hair, cut from my virgin head, rotting away in my parents' freezer. I never turned them into extensions. My mother saved them, like dried roses, for no good reason at all.

That night, I dreamed of the hairs forming a tight braid around my throat, squeezing the breath out of me. I woke up, disappointed to be alive.

⚡

How do I tell you the story of the worst bet I ever made? Do I tell it from the end to the front, from the point where I knew how catastrophically I had failed? Or should I start it from the beginning, when I knew the least I would ever know?

I can't remember much about my wedding, which other women—onetime brides, longtime wives—told me was normal. When you're engaged, other women who've done it too start to bombard you with advice, whether you ask for it or not. Everywhere I went, there was someone who had had a wedding, who wanted to tell me what to prepare for. *Everything will be a blur. You're not going to get to eat a thing. You're hardly going to remember who came. Make sure you write down who gave you gifts, that'll be tough to remember, too. It's going to be the greatest day of your life! Don't worry if you don't have sex that night, you'll be exhausted. You're never going to eat any of the cake. You need less alcohol than you think! You won't think about how you look; you'll only care about how you feel. Bring flat shoes so you can dance!* There's something covert about being a fiancée, the way everyone else who's ever held the title wants to share a little wisdom, a little tidbit. There was an internal language to it, like how "let me see your ring" is a prompt for you to ask to see *her* ring, or how the correct response to someone saying their wedding date is April 20 is apparently not, "Oh, that's Hitler's birthday."

Some of what the other brides told me was true—I don't remember much about my wedding day, or *days*, as it were. I remember running my fingers across the scalloped edge of my wedding lehenga. I remember how much I loved the stitching. I remember how my ex-husband started the day with a freak allergic reaction. He bought a tempeh and tomato sandwich instead of the BLT he thought he was buying. An hour before our ceremony, his face was fat and red and puffy, his lips like a Joe Sacco illustration. He was mortified; I thought it was sweet and held his face in my hands in our photos before the ceremony started.

"This isn't very auspicious," he said to me, hangdog about his appearance. "Auspicious" is the word Indians use a thousand times at weddings, to denote how blessed a union is. The food's arrival was auspicious. Our star charts showed a good match: also auspicious. The fact that he was cheating on me but I had no idea? I'm sure someone would find a way to make it work in our favor.

I remember our engagement much more clearly. We were in London for a week in 2016, visiting my ex's friend. The friend was about to turn forty, bruised from his recent divorce that I thought was mostly his fault. We arrived at his house, and I was jet-lagged and exhausted. I didn't want to go out. "We just got here, can't we relax?" I asked my ex while a ring burned a hole in his pocket.

He persuaded me to have two glasses of champagne, and by the time we ambled over to St. Katharine Docks, I was sleepy and drunk and silly. "Hold on," I told him as I tumbled toward a classic red English phone booth. "I'm going to take a photo of this and send it to Robert." Robert worked for my publisher, and was the only British person I knew, so I had big plans to walk around London sending him photos of attractions with stupid comments. "I found your watch," I wrote to him with a photo of Big Ben. "Did you leave your phone here?" I wrote with a photo of the phone booth. I had blocked out my calendar for the next day to find some bald Britons to secretly photograph to send to Robert as well. "Is this your brother?" is what I had planned to say, six or seven times in a row.

When I spun back around from the phone booth, laughing at my own cleverness, my ex was already crying and fiddling with something in his pocket. He held the ring aloft, a ruby encircled by diamonds.

"Yes?" he asked me, as I welled up with tears that surprised me. I nodded. "Well, then put it on already," he said, laughing, crying, *god, we were so happy*. I put the ring on and felt unsettled, even if I was excited at the same time. I wasn't surprised by the proposal—I mean, I designed the ring, I'm not insane enough to leave such a big decision to a straight man who wore pageboy hats and wanted to get me, an ethnic, a *white gold band*—but even as I felt one burden lift, I knew a new one would settle in after it.

Our engagement was largely designed to solve one main problem: my father hadn't spoken to me in a year by that point. Once loquacious, calling me daily and offering little updates on his day-to-day—"I'm making slushees," he used to say to me, in reference to the single banana smoothie he had made weeks prior, *and hated*—he cut off all contact with me when he found out I was living with someone. We were unmarried and cohabiting, a rebellion my dad couldn't tolerate. I missed him. He never asked how I was anymore. When I called and he picked up the phone, he would brusquely mutter something about finding my mother, and hand her the phone without sticking around to listen in on our conversation. I'd come back to this feeling it gave me, this total emptiness, to go from hearing from him daily to his utter lack of interest in my life because of one decision. Later, when I'd wonder if maybe it was time to call a divorce lawyer, I'd return to how this felt: Could I do it again if my dad decided I didn't exist, one more time?

These days, Papa and I don't discuss the lost year, though we do talk about nearly everything else. It's too common in our family for a couple of relatives to stop speaking for a while, a little cold war, until someone thaws or until someone dies or until someone forgets. One of my uncles didn't speak to my aunty for a year because she didn't say hello to him at a party. Another hasn't spoken to anyone in the family for reasons that have never been made clear, but he does call my mom every few years, as if to give her false hope before taking it away yet again. My dad and I have just moved on, pretending as if I didn't have to get Ontario's marriage license board involved to get him to talk to me on the phone again.

I knew getting engaged, and making my relationship real to him, would mean Papa would warm up. My ex was ready to get married; it felt inevitable, and for a little while it felt like the exact right choice. My ex was once so earnest in how much he loved me. I took it for granted, and by the time I noticed it was gone, well, it was gone.

———

"You don't think it would be nice?" he would murmur into my ear, years before we got married. "Don't you want to be with me forever?" These were the good, salient questions. What other answers were there? Yes, it would be nice. Yes, I wanted to be with him forever. He'd rest a warm, flat palm on my heart and curl his body around me from behind while we lay in bed. But in my mind's eye, above all else: it's what my mother wanted.

Papa stopped talking to me because I wasn't married, but I felt my mother's grief palpitate when we talked about how I wasn't giving her a wedding to plan. For most of her life, she's been stuck as the mediator for the rest of us. She stands between my brother and me, siblings twelve years apart in age, with no middle ground to be found. She stands between us and our dad, who always has some little grievance, some nit to be picked. The latest is his television's sound system. "HOW do you USE this BLOODY THING," he bellows, one of several different kinds of yells he has. Bellowing is for objects, screaming for traffic, barking for children, and grumbling for wives. Strangers do not get any of this. Instead, they are forced to tolerate something much spookier: my father's dull, affectless rendition of, "I don't see how this is my problem."

So, it wasn't just that he stopped speaking to me. My mother was collateral damage in his grief over my refusal to play by his rules. "I always knew you wouldn't have an arranged marriage like me," she told me once, "but *this*?" She said *this* while waving her hands broadly but dismissively across our laps as we sat facing each other on the couch, our legs crossed and our knees touching, like we normally do. *This* was the age difference between us. *This* was how white he was. *This* was how I moved in with him before getting married. *This* was how I made it seem like getting married wouldn't be anyone else's choice but mine.

I know, I *know*. To white people, or to people with freer families, it sounds silly to suggest marriage would be anyone else's decision. But Indian families operate by committee. Everyone gets a vote, even if all votes aren't counted equally. My parents always asked me what I wanted, even if my feelings were ignored. We were heard, but not respected. And so it was a surprise to them both that I didn't ask for counsel. "This has always been your problem," my mother said, sadly but with a frisson of pleasure. "Always saying sorry. Never asking for permission."

My choices isolated my mother, too. How could she show her face to the other aunties, who were busy with new grandchildren and comfortable retirement? My mother always believed in her own good karma: she got an education, married someone her father liked, followed her husband to Canada, and raised two awful, ungrateful, brutal little children into self-effacing, criminally insecure adults. To her, marrying me off meant she had succeeded. Marrying me off meant she could relax. "Don't you want me to die at peace?" she used to say, her first and only retort to get me and my brother to do something we didn't want to do. "I'm not going to be here forever. Don't you want to make me happy?"

———

One of my earliest memories is of wrapping myself around my mother's leg at the age of three while she stood at the kitchen counter, flattening atta into discs, dropping them onto the naked element of the stove with her bare fingers. "Mom, can you have another baby?" I asked her, touching her stomach with the same easy permission that I touched my own. "I don't like having an older brother. I want a little sister." I don't know why I remember this conversation; it reveals little other than how tenuous my grasp of human reproduction was (and would continue to be until an age too humiliating to admit in print). But I remember it because my mom looked down at me and smiled the way she does when she knows more than me. She looked at me like she knew time would correct me: one day, I'd understand just how enormous this request was.

"I don't think I can have any more babies, but I can ask God for one more and see what he says," my mom, forty by that point, told me gently. I remember how warm and big her body felt to me, like she could stop a bullet merely by looking at it disapprovingly and asking it where its parents were. But even at that age, I knew she was smiling at me because she understood something I didn't. I knew I had asked for something impossible but she didn't want to take away my hope.

"Don't you want to make me happy?" my mom asked me as an adult. I smiled at her the way she had smiled at me: she didn't know what I knew, that marriage would not solve anything for either of us. She wanted to marry me off so that I would be taken care of, but I knew my soon-to-be husband was not the nurturing type. And much like she had done at my brother's wedding, my mother fainted at mine too, though not because of radical dieting. She was just stressed out. She fainted in front of a roaring fire, held up by my cousins who were crushing sugar cubes and pressing granules onto her tongue. "She'll be fine, her blood sugar is a bit low," Neeta said, dribbling apple juice into my mother's gaping maw. "Just finish the ceremony."

When my mother asked if I wanted her to be happy, if I could just give her this one little thing, I smiled at my mother because I didn't want to ruin her optimism. I smiled because it was sweet, the way she thought it was so simple.

Even before I got engaged, before I got married, long before I'd check into a hotel room in Bushwick while I looked for my own apartment and my hair would start falling out and my skin would break into rashes and I would have nightmares about my mother casting me out of her home again and again and again, I knew this wasn't the right choice.

It was something she'd learn in due time. Why ruin her day? So, I smiled. In that way, she was right, and would always be right: I wanted to make her happy.

⚡

My jaw aches when I think about my wedding—all four days of it. It's a poisonous mix of embarrassment and nausea, of getting carsick in a cab stuck on the BQE while you realize you texted the wrong person a piece of reckless and salacious gossip. It's like thinking back to your preteen talent show performance, something I decided to do before I realized I wasn't that talented. I just wasn't very good at marriage, and yet I dared try it with a big ceremony and an endless reception. It was an event witnessed by nearly everyone I have ever known in my entire life, and now, in my divorce, by several people I'll never speak to again.

There's another version of this essay living somewhere in another universe. In that one, we stayed together. In that one, I am still a wife, and I have plenty of thoughts on what being a wife means. I am happy, and so is he. No one feels like a failure. My parents still get to proudly talk about their married children, how we're both "taken care of." Maybe I have a baby, bare gums and dark hair—we look at the baby and play-fight about who the baby looks more like. (This is a waste of time; the baby looks more like me because I am the one with the dominant genes. But because I am a kind and generous and patient wife, just like my mother, I let him pretend that our baby even remotely looks like him, with my big nose, and my brown eyes, and my black hair, and our shared birthmark that looks like a scar from a stab wound.) In the mornings, my husband still wakes me up by tickling the inside of my arm with his beard. At night, he still complains that I'm keeping the lights on reading when he wants to go to bed. It's a nice alternate reality that I visit from time to time, like my taking a drive up the coast on a breezy Saturday (I can't drive) or pretending like climate change isn't going to burn my corneas out by the time I'm fifty.

My wedding lasted a week, with my entire extended family descending upon Toronto, two weeks before my husband and I would be moving to New York. My bua FaceTimed my chacha into our ceremony, holding him aloft so everyone could see this brown guy in a white tank top reclining in bed and heckling me on my wedding day. A family of raccoons broke into our apartment the night before our wedding, terrorizing my future mother-in-law who had to shoo them out of the house while my cat—some apex predator she is— watched with passive interest. Our Pandit was the most memorable part of our wedding, only because I fucking hated him. My parents wanted an old-world touch in our considerably "modern" wedding—I wasn't taking my husband's last name, our reception was *aggressively* open bar, plus I had refused to be carried to the pyre by one of my uncles. (Though, upon further reflection, none of my septuagenarian uncles were dying to heft 175 pounds over their shoulder toward a roaring fire.) Pandit-Ji was a senior citizen built like a wire, who lectured my future husband and me about the value of a Hindu marriage above a Christian one. Our first meeting with him should have scared me off—he spent most of it quizzing my white fiancé on whether he was ready to marry "in the Hindu fashion." But he checked the imaginary boxes my parents invented for the occasion. My father has never been religious, and yet on this, he was strident: "Make sure you find a good Pandit."

In any case, I'm only telling you all this because I wrote it down. I squirrelled notes away about the wedding week as it unfolded, on the tossed envelopes of cash gifts, on receipts for alterations of my dress, on my thigh while I was on the phone with the wholesaler who made my Parvati and Shiva centerpieces. I can only remember the details in this forced hindsight, where my own words are a map for what I lived, and yet can't fully recall.

Even if you don't believe in the pomp of a wedding, it's hard to deny the little thrills you get when you lean into the ceremony of it. I felt like a woman the first time sindoor was applied to the part of my hair, my mother's finger rubbing it into my scalp. The red powder is one of a few visual markers Indian women get and perform to show the world they're married—to stop wearing it is to suggest widowhood. *Maybe I'll start wearing sindoor every day*, I thought. I imagined myself like the mothers and wives in Bollywood movies at the beginning of the first act: Busying herself in the kitchen with chai and roti, pulling her dupatta back over her head every time it slips, bowing piously at the portrait of her dead in-laws in the living room. I could be this woman. I could pretend.

I had an engagement ring and two thin gold bands on my left hand, but what felt more foreign were the earrings and my gold-and-black necklace, two especially Kashmiri markers of a woman who just got married. Indians could tell I was a new bride from afar. "Your mangalsutra," a waiter said to me once, pointing with his eyes to my neckline while his hands were full of dosa. "Very nice." Mangalsutra means "auspicious thread," an indicator to the world that I'm married, but also protection for myself as a married woman. It was a cue to others that billions of women before me had displayed in another era: someone loves me enough to cover me in gold.

These were symbols and objects for me to keep. Crossing over the threshold into married life was a rite of passage into adulthood. I would be gifted talismans to protect me in this next phase of life. When you have a bar mitzvah, or a quinceañera, or a baptism, you walk through the elements and emerge transformed: now, you are an adult, or saved, or otherwise metamorphosed. Butterflies don't go back to being caterpillars.

How would we get the sindoor out of my hair if this marriage didn't work? I worried that a committee of married women would come to my door in the future, hearing about my marital discord. They'd be holding the sindoor container my mom still has, the one I always admired and hoped to own one day: a small, silver swan, its wing opening just enough for your ring finger to press inside. The aunties would force me down into a chair, and brush the sindoor back into the swan, shave the top of my head, and lock me away. "Such a shame," they'd say in Hindi and Kashmiri and Urdu and Punjabi. "*Tsk tsk tsk.* You were such a beautiful bride."

My niece walked me down the aisle wearing a green dress that she found itchy but tolerated for my sake. "Thank you," I said to her, holding her hand, and she nodded through her bravery—the dress was indeed a huge imposition. I waited to join my soon-to-be husband at the altar while listening to the Pandit make jokes at my expense. "They say that when a woman marries a man, she gains a great deal of knowledge, getting her own degrees in life," he said, waving his long arms around like a spider I wanted to kill. "When a woman marries, after all, she gains a master's." My guests groaned, and I suppose I was briefly grateful that I wasn't friends with a bunch of fucking losers who thought this was funny.

Traditionally, in Hindu homes, you become the property of the man's side of the family when you marry. Your last name changes, you move in with your in-laws, and whatever ties bound you to your parents are essentially cut. The wedding itself is a severance; the weddings take days, in part, because everyone wants you to be sure. You can't go home again, so you ought to be sure. Men don't have the same rules; they continue to live with and see their families.

Everything given to you is about protecting you from bad faith or your husband's rebellion. The gold your family drapes around your neck is financial security; in case he abandons you. The blessings given to you are about fertility and joy, but above all, that you and your partner continue to work as a team. The hope isn't so much that you don't suffer—Kashmiris appreciate, nay, *love* suffering—but just that you never have to do it alone. It's a nice gesture. I believed, once, that our families could protect us from forthcoming harm just by walking us to the altar. I believed we were building a new framework where we would be partnered in our tragedies and in our successes. It was true for my mother, so I wanted it to be true for me, too.

The darker your mehndi turns, the more your future husband loves you. Mine ran burgundy and all my aunties cooed over my hands and feet, as if it was proof that I had made an auspicious choice. The poojas, too, were about sending me off. The week of the wedding, I was covered in honey and milk as a way of setting me up for luck in a new life, far away from my own blood. My family enrobed me in gold, theirs and mine, a protection from future ill will. My aunties kissed the top of my head. My uncles got quiet and muttered something about how I was once so small, I could fit in their pockets. Everyone was getting ready to let me go.

My ex and I were tied together with a chunni used by all my older cousins at their weddings, and instructed to walk around the agni seven times. Each step—a sphere—is a single promise to each other: to be responsible to each other, to gain spiritual strength, to increase our combined wealth, to learn, to raise a family, to live long together, to be committed only to each other. It was so hot that my makeup was melting, my hands and feet so slippery I was worried I'd fall into the fire. I finished the rituals in as perfunctory a manner as I could. I didn't like how I felt in my dress, I didn't like how hot I was, I loathed the Pandit and everything he said. I was frustrated even by the one moment of the ceremony we thought we could control: our witness signatures. My ex wanted his own best friend to do it, and I chose Baby Braga, but when the time came, the Pandit called up our siblings without consulting us. We were too tired and frozen in our confusion to pick a fight in front of 180 guests, most of whom were white and had no idea things were going wrong even when they were. My brother walked up to the altar and raised his hands in the air in victory, like a wrestler who had just pinned his opponent with a metal chair. Our guests rooted for him, as I stood behind him. "What the fuck is this?" I said, largely for myself, because everyone was cheering too loudly to hear me.

Our wedding ceremony was supposed to last thirty minutes; it took more than an hour. The Pandit failed to announce a first kiss, and so I turned to my new husband, grabbed his face, and kissed him anyway. In the photos, the Pandit's hand is on my shoulder, trying to pull me off. Parvati stomps her feet; she gets what she wants.

We signed the paperwork at the altar quickly, desperate to spill out onto the street for a few stolen moments away from our guests before the reception. I hugged my new in-laws, his sister, my dad. But before we could leave, my mother pulled me in for a hug in the corner of the altar. She whispered in my ear and hugged me like I was something she was letting go of forever. It's the only moment of my life that felt too long, and yet not long enough. Like if I could stay there, everything wouldn't go wrong later. Our audience stopped talking, stopped cheering. We created silence big enough for just the two of us to live in. I forgot my husband was even there.

When he and I ran back down the aisle with our friends throwing flower petals (I think? I'm not actually sure. It sounds like something that might have happened), my husband skipped down the steps and into the street with ebullience. "We did it!" he said, referring to the big It. We had won my family over, we had fought against all odds, and now we were together forever. *We* did it. We *did* it.

"The Pandit was horrible," I said. "Those jokes. And we had the wrong witnesses. And you didn't want your parents sitting together but he made them and—" I started to tear up, thinking about all the little things that went wrong.

"Who cares?" he said. "We're married. That's all we wanted." He ran his thumb across my face, brushing away the small tear that started to bead on my cheek. He was the happiest I had seen him. It felt like we would never have to fight with anyone or anything again in our lives. "What did your mom say in there, when she hugged you? It looked intense." Later, at our reception, when I had changed into a black gown and more gold than before and kicked my shoes off, more people would ask me what she said in my ear during that hug. "It was the only time you cried during the whole ceremony," a friend said to me, laughing. "Whatever it was, it must have been good."

I demurred. "It wasn't in English," I said. "It's tough to translate from Kashmiri. It's an inside joke." I didn't feel like explaining what she'd said, how it felt like a promise that I could come back home if I needed to. I didn't want anyone else to know how I could tell that after all *that*—all the fighting, the pleas for my case, the strident belief that *he is the one*—she wasn't that sure about this marriage either. She held me, and I felt her anxiety shoot back into my body. In that nanosecond, we traded all our worries.

"Wherever you go," she told me, quietly, so quiet I had to strain to hear, "just make sure you're happy. Even if I can't go with you. Make sure you're happy." It was like leaving a light on and the door unlocked for someone you're not sure is ever coming back. I held her words against my chest for years, protecting them like a lantern running out of oil, like my last chance to get back home.

⚡

Mom has always been physically weaker than my dad. I can split my childhood up into phases of her ailing health. There was the arthritis phase, where her pain was so intense in her elbow and ribs that I knew it was a bad day based on how much time she needed with a heating pad. There was the fainting phase, where her thyroid stopped cooperating around the time she went on another crash diet that left her with too few calories to burn. Her pregnancy with me was a phase unto itself: Having already had a fallopian tube removed, my mother went to the doctor for her checkup before a needed hysterectomy. The surgery had to be canceled because she was pregnant.

And yet! I used to be afraid of my mother, this tiny woman whose hands are so small she needs both of them to operate a regular-sized cup. Sometimes she still scares me, even in her physical absence. There's a Caribbean woman in my neighborhood who goes to the grocery store at the same time as me, every week. When I hear her bangles shift down her arm when she's reaching for peas, I shiver. That *clink* sounds like my mother raising a hand (or a spoon or a slipper or the top of a Tupperware container) to hit me on the arm and tell me to get out of her way.

I was afraid of this tiny woman, this little doll who gave birth to me and has been shrinking ever since. The one I never feared was my dad. Papa was our patriarch, yes, and we had been conditioned to view him as the head of our four-person family, but to fear him was to be afraid of shadowboxing. He was all bark, even if he was bark most of the time. Even now, my mom sometimes calls me to make me listen to *her* yell at *him*. "This isn't for you," she said on the phone to me, taking a brief pause from screaming at my father, "but you need to listen to me tell him he's being stupid."

Despite the hierarchy of my parents' marriage, and namely that they were auspiciously introduced through family friends, it seems odd that I didn't have a model for shutting my mouth and listening to my husband, allowing him to guide our family. I have never heard my mom shut up once in my life. I have never seen my father wield any kind of power over her. Growing up, Papa was a hothead who had plenty of opinions, but most of them could be easily brushed away or mitigated by a joke about his barely-under-control hoarding. Mom made our lunches and bought our clothes and knew our friends and set the rules. Mom knew when I was lying. Papa had no power over anyone, especially not our mother. What was his plan? Get angry with her and hope that she would still pack his lunchtime tiffin with two roti, one container of aloo gobi, another of monj haakh, that she'd still feed him with care? No: Papa is suitably afraid of her, too, living on the margins of her affection, happy if she's willing to give him a few morsels that day. He doesn't do much to win her affections, but he's careful not to alienate her too much.

"I need her more than she needs me," he told me once, in the waiting room at the hospital, while we waited for her to wake up. He said it with an undertone I never wanted to hear again: *What will we do if she doesn't wake up?*

The pandemic landed in New York a few months after my first wedding anniversary, after our cursed trip to Hudson where I would cry and wonder how our marriage had gone so wrong, so soon. My parents were in India, and would end up stranded there for months. Twice a day, I'd FaceTime them at my uncle's house with no updates on how I'd get them home. In turn, I'd be faced with two different narratives. "You need to DO something," my mother would hiss at me, hunched over in another room away from our relatives, as if she had just missed the last helicopter out of Saigon. "I can't cook in Chachi's kitchen anymore. She's such a control freak. She made just five eggs for four people! Who cooks like that? I hate it here. Call the airline! Call the government! We are Canadian citizens, they can't just let us DIE here!"

My father, meanwhile, was being tended to the way the eldest brother and oldest husband would, in India at least. "Ah, it's not so bad," he said languorously after my mother had become so verklempt that she could no longer speak to me. "I'm with my brother, I'm with my sister. We haven't been together like this since we were kids! I can't complain." He swished around amber liquid in a rocks glass, holding it up to the camera. "You see this? Double malt." He started laughing. "'Double malt. Double malt!' I don't even know what that means!"

I watched my mother get frail over FaceTime. She was taking a steady dose of hydroxychloroquine for her arthritis, the very drug that the forty-fifth President of these Free and Glorious United States had been saying was a cure for

Covid-19. It wasn't, but that didn't stop India's pharmacies from shipping much of their stock over to the US, where demand was predictably booming. She got weaker, her pain more acute. Even when I found a surgeon who was able to drive over several doses of the drug to her place in a rural township far north, I worried she would return to me in a state of irreversible fragility.

By the time she made it back to Canada, two months later, it didn't seem like her current bout of frailty would swerve into a bounce-back. But this is a common experience—no one has found the cure for having to watch our parents get older. And once she came back home, it was clear that her joints would be the first in several hurdles she'd have to leap over in the years to come. I'd have to return home for three weeks to help take care of her after a knee replacement; following her surgery, she would need help in the shower, the bathroom. She would need someone to hold her hand. Later, when she was at her sickest, I'd press the pads of my fingers into the pads of hers. "Imagine if you got that hysterectomy and didn't end up having me," I told her. "You'd be stuck with Bhaiya. *And* Papa. Mom, you'd be suck with *Bhaiya* and *Papa*."

Her eyes bulged while she shook her head. "I *know*."

I had to explain my departure to my husband first. Her surgery would disrupt our Christmas plans, and was sched-uled between the holidays and a long work trip that would further keep me away from our shared home. But this wasn't optional, which I made clear to him while I looked for flights to take me home within the week.

"Fine. Whatever," he said, rolling his eyes. "Do what you want, like you always do."

"It's not like I'm going on vacation." I thought about how suffocating Calgary can be: I was gearing up to reenter my childhood home, now filled with illness and seclusion instead of my mom frying zeera and cloves at two in the afternoon.

"It's not like you asked me for permission," he said, leaving the room. "You've already decided to leave."

On her second day post-op, my mother made it up the winding staircase in their home. It was more hectic than it needed to be, with my dad hopping around us, unable to help but more than happy to just keep talking. "Lift your leg like this," he'd say, jerking his leg into a shape that wouldn't even make sense for a healthy person. "Use your glutes! Lift your body with your thighs!"

My mother wept and wailed into my shoulder and bargained with me instead. "Can't I do this tomorrow? Can't I just wait a little longer?"

I told her she couldn't, and so I glued my leg to hers and we learned to walk up the stairs together. "Papa, *move*," I snarled at my dad who remained a quarter-inch from my mother's legs at all times, throwing her off-balance. He brought her a chair to sit in when she got to the top, fourteen grueling steps that left us both drenched in sweat. She was panting and proud, and I knelt at her feet. She pulled me forward by my collar, brusquely, the way she did when I was little and had accidentally let the word "fuck" slither out of my mouth. A yank, and my face was an inch from hers. She kissed me on the forehead.

"I didn't know I could do that," she said once she caught her breath. She took a shower, largely on her own, and I had never seen her so proud of her own body before.

My spouse was right. I would never ask his permission to go home. It wasn't his permission to give.

⚡

Papa wanted to help with Mom's recovery, but he was quite literally helpless. My mother is the backbone of our family, the only person that everyone can get along with. What a joyless position to be in. She manages the dynamics of three lugubrious, unruly churls who cope well neither with each other nor with outsiders. My mom is a Disney princess with three trolls following her around. My mom is Marge Simpson, her kids and loaf husband all useless without her guide. At her funeral, you'll catch me pretending like she never did anything wrong in her life, screaming like an Italian tough guy, "Don't say a word about my mother! My mother was a SAINT!"

In order to do a fraction of what my mother did in the house, I returned home for three weeks and tried to do the cooking and the laundry. I had no problem fulfilling my father's idiotic breakfast demands: exactly fourteen soaked almonds with a slop of overripe papaya and two slices of burned toast. What troubled me was the forty-minute argument that ensued because I did not want to share a breakfast of an identical fourteen soaked almonds with a slop of overripe papaya and two slices of burned toast. He couldn't understand it: My mother ate it every day, so why couldn't I? Her medication turned her appetite all the way off, and so she was briefly exempt from their ritual. "But I don't want fourteen soaked almonds with a slop of overripe papaya and two slices of burned toast, Papa," I told him. He looked like I had just told him about a goblin I knew who had recently been indicted on charges of tax evasion.

I wanted to be patient with him but I wasn't. I finally snapped when he sprinkled no fewer than nineteen dollars' worth of walnuts on a cherry tomato and sausage pasta I had made us. And look, I know you're here to read about more salient things, about something devastating and poignant maybe. But I think we'd all be remiss if we didn't pause for a moment to discuss the fact that my father put a bunch of fucking nuts on a meat pasta. Sure, maybe a pine nut makes sense, even a pistachio in some contexts. But raw, unpeeled walnuts, papery skin still attached?

"You were designed in a lab to drive me insane," I told him, still wearing my mother's apron, holding a wooden spoon aloft, *desperate* to hit him in the head with it.

"I don't see how this is my problem," he said, pouring a quarter-cup of chili crisp atop his nut-meat-pasta pile.

My older brother moved back into the house for the rest of my trip, to fill the space between my father's demands ("Can you make salmon with broccoli? We don't have any fish but maybe you can just make it with chicken.") and my mother's medical needs. It was the first time since I was twelve that the four of us were back in the same house together. During the day, my brother and I worked in separate rooms, pretending that our respective jobs mattered while my mother tried to wiggle her way out of physiotherapy. We only came together to fight. My brother would intervene when my dad was getting on my nerves; my brother calmly explained to my mother why she had to bend and flex and stretch her leg fifteen times, twice a day; my brother would tell me to "stop crying," and somehow that would be enough to get me to cut it out.

I looked at the way my brother's shoulder sloped when he walked. Our parents' mortalities are starting to face us more now, they're starting to get a little louder now, and my brother and I are forced to meet as adults in this way. When we were children, it was easier to please them: he would perform well in school as the academically gifted one, and I'd write a poem or draw a picture or do a dance and be given a pat on the head. These days, neither of us can make them happy like we did as kids, and so a wedding was my last chance at giving my mom what she wanted. Maybe, finally, she would feel satiated by my efforts. This was the biggest show of dedication to her that I had left: I would tie myself to a man, for her.

The older we get, the more it feels like we're raising our own parents. "You have to talk to Mom," I'll call my brother to complain about how she won't just take a fucking edible to help with her chronic pain. "Can you deal with Papa?" he'll implore of me over text, after he got in an argument with our dad over his medically required veganism. Our parents are the only place we see each other.

Do our childhood archetypes matter anymore? My brother

was Good and I was Bad. He was born in India and brought here as a toddler; he thrived and has overachieved. He married well and gave my parents a grandchild and works the right job and keeps tidy, short fingernails. I was born in Canada as a complete surprise. My brother was already fully a person, whereas I was a screaming mass, which I still am. My brother is stoic and emotionally complex. I am chatty and emotionally competent. Together, our brains might make one healthy person.

After a particularly hard day—Mom's pain at a nine, refusing to eat, sobbing raggedly as I gingerly extended her leg up, two-three-four, and down, two-three-four—I crawled into bed like it was the soft landing of defeat. Every day, I watched my mother get older, joylessly. Her recovery felt like a precursor for life without her; me, devastated, my dad and brother these distant planets orbiting around, never getting close enough for comfort.

One afternoon, my mother grabbed me by the collar again and pulled my ear toward her lips. "Can you stay an extra week?" she asked. "Just one more week. If your husband says no, it's okay—"

I cut her off. "I don't need permission." I extended my trip, and took his call in another room. It was loud enough, my mother told me later, that she could hear every word.

Later that night, my brother knocked on the door to his old bedroom, now my old bedroom. "Do you want some?" he asked, shaking an orange container full of weed he had brought me to calm my frayed edges. "It's mellow."

I followed him into the bathroom we used to share as kids. I packed the one-hitter for myself, cracked the window open, and closed the door. I smoked in silence while he watched me. I was exhausted, slumped against the lip of the tub. When was the last time we had been in this bathroom together? 2001? There was still the epilator Mom had bought for my legs, the hair gel he used back when he went to high school. We were sitting in a time capsule.

"Do you know what Papa called my friend Lakna the other day?" I told him, forever trying to get him to engage with me on something, anything.

"What?"

"First, he called her Noreen. Then, he called her Lakania. And then, for half the day, he called her Dilmo."

"Where did he get Dilmo from?" my brother asked, playing with a plastic comb from another century.

"I have no idea. He knew it was wrong but he couldn't stop saying it. He was wandering around the house muttering 'Dilmo' to himself for hours and getting frustrated with himself."

"That reminds me of what David Letterman used to call Jimmy Fallon when he started in late night," he said. We were a Letterman house; there was no Leno to be seen, and that bias quietly extended to Fallon, too. ("Nonsense," my father would say to the variety show elements of his programming, while my mom blushed watching his little white body dance on-screen. "He's so cute," she'd say in delight, wiggling her finger at him from the couch. "Like a little gnome.")

"What did Letterman call him?" I asked my brother, clicking the lighter.

"Lonnie Donegan."

My brother buckled over in howling laughter and we both teared up, gasping for air, clutching our sides, trying to not disturb our sleeping parents. I cried, which was what I did most of the time back then, but hid it with another puff. This all felt like a precursor to death—Mom's, ours, who knew—but what a comfort to laugh in the face of the devil with someone made of your own sinew and salt.

We retreated to our own bedrooms, and watched the Lonnie Donegan skit on our respective phones. I heard his laugh ricochet. I felt braver.

My mother started to improve, and so I decided to return to New York, to my marriage. My brother drove me to the airport for the first time. Usually my parents took me, trip after trip, but getting my mother in a car was an undertaking, and my parents would rather do things in a pair if they have to do them at all. (I did too, once.) In the car, my brother asked me about my husband, who he barely knew. "He's really . . . emotional," he said. "He seems very in tune with his feelings."

I thought about grabbing his arm and stopping him from getting on the highway to Calgary's airport. I could tell him I was in trouble, that my marriage wasn't working, that if I went back to New York it might break for good. My husband was emotional, yes—I was feeling less and less equipped to deal with his feelings, which were big and loud and starting to scare me. I thought about begging him for help—he was always my de facto third parent, and was sure to have an answer that Mom or Papa didn't. I thought about telling him about how annihilated I felt as a wife. I thought about telling him I felt trapped. My brother had helped me before. I just had to ask. I just had to ask him for help.

I nodded in the passenger seat. "Yes, he feels very deeply," I said. "Not like us."

⚡

My mother's knee surgery crystallized something for me, even if I was unable to identify it at the time. My dad was her useless companion but he was her *companion*. I ridiculed his inability to take care of her while showing any patience, but the point was that my dad was trying to take care of her. He monitored her medication to make sure she didn't take too many or too few Oxys, just enough so that she could build her strength back up. He ensured she ate three meals a day, even when she refused, when she cried that even eating took too much energy. She slept on the guest bed brought down to the living room, and so he slept on the couch next to her the whole time. My dad is a menace to society, and often to my mother, but he's a present menace. He was *there*. I didn't feel like I had the same companionship.

But then again, my parents' marriage exemplified all the things I didn't want in my own, all the things I was getting anyway. I had long accepted the realities of my parents' marriage: My mother was always going to make dinner and clean the house and remember our birthdays, and my father was always going to work and handle the finances and keep us at a generous and thankful emotional remove. That didn't mean I wanted it for myself. Unlike the women in my family generations before me—all of them, every single one—I didn't want to be married just for the sake of being married. It wasn't a prize. It was a fait accompli before it even happened: the Koul girls all get married, and they stay married.

There had only been a few times in our marriage when I discussed divorce, and my husband knew the trump card well: "How will you tell your parents?" He knew I couldn't, he knew it was too shaming and too huge to tell them. I would always stay and always try to make it work.

Later, I'd overhear my brother further explaining my divorce to my parents, the way he did every time I fucked up at school. "She failed one math test, she isn't going to become a vagrant," he said in 1999. "She got suspended for three days. She's not going to prison, Mom. That other girl just needs to learn to keep her hands to herself," he said in 2005. "Think about how bad it had to be for her to leave. Think about what she won't tell you," he said in 2022.

A month after my mother's surgery, I was back in New York, holding my crushed marriage in my hand like an origami crane, stepped on and discarded. Within days, I was temporarily staying in my friend Kelly's apartment in Park Slope while I figured out what to do next. Her railroad-style apartment was a perfect place for me to hide. For a month, I paced from her kitchen all the way to her bedroom, crying so hard that her neighbors could hear and would periodically make fun of me by mimicking my wailing. Kelly was on vacation, and left me for a time with her dog, Leslie Stahl, a hefty and mercurial cognac-colored Shiba mix who kept me alive by pushing her snout into my neck when I cried in her mother's bed. I brought an insane mix of things to Kelly's apartment: mismatched clothes that weren't appropriate for the weather, several Lucite earrings, and a facial toning machine my husband (ex-husband?) had given me. I don't know why I packed like that. I've never been good in a crisis.

I called my parents to tell them, keeping the conversation as short as possible. Two of my female cousins would do the rest of the work for me, and soon the majority of my family would know within a week or so. (You really do have to give gossips credit for keeping the world and the word moving.)

My family doesn't keep secrets. That would suggest we have the capacity for privacy at all. Everyone in the family knows about every stupid thing I've ever done—if my parents were determined to tell everyone the details of my middle school suspension, they would surely be determined to tell everyone about my divorce, to handle the messaging themselves, to spare me the indignity of admitting, "He was white, he was old, and he was the wrong choice." Was it that simple? It didn't matter; they needed something pat and clear, and would explain it to themselves and each other in whatever way worked best.

After I told my parents that I would soon be their divorced daughter I hid in shame from them all. This has been the most frustrating part of divorce for me: it's fucking embarrassing. You spent tens upon tens of thousands of dollars on a party dedicated to bragging about how in love you are, how sure you are in this forever-choice, only to be wrong? To hide away at your friend's apartment with a dog who won't stop pooping next to the Peloton?

A wedding—an Indian wedding in particular—is a declaration of a woman's independence through a new dependence. That's the root of what marriage has historically been for women. Without the means or ability to work freely, to swim upstream alone against capitalism and colonialism, we needed husbands to help us move out and up. Marriages were property agreements; weddings were proof of a family's wealth, and their ability to create powerful land and financial deals through their children. As we modernized, weddings became proclamations not of love, but of being *chosen*. My Indian wedding was a loud shout, a brag that I had finally been chosen as worthy enough to be loved. So many of our rites and rituals are tied to marriage—and isn't that odd? Why wait to bestow heirlooms until your offspring meets someone they want to be with "forever": blue earrings, beloved dresses. Only once I was cast out of my family into my husband's did my family start to cover my spirit with gold. They were sending me away, so I needed to be protected from new and unforeseen forces. It never felt optional to be sent away in the first place.

Now, I had effectively asked to come home, and was humiliated by my own regression. It felt like I couldn't hack it in the real world. It was all very *I'm already a burden to my parents and I'm frightened*. After telling my parents the truth, I ignored their follow-up calls and considered what a life fully and truly alone might feel like. You only get to leave home once.

Our family always considered me the crier in our group. This, I think, is unfair: I was the crier because I was a child when everyone else was an adult. I still don't like crying in front of my family, but when my brother called me over FaceTime, I answered mid-sob without really thinking about it.

My brother heard about my divorce quickly after my parents did, and he called me—a rare occurrence. When his neutral face appeared on my laptop, I thought about how he had acted as my witness at my wedding, in my victory, and would do the same in my grief. He'd report back to my parents that I was worse off than I even appeared. I didn't want to be tattled on like he might have done when we were children.

He was eating attentively when he called. He's a very tidy eater. It drives me nuts. "So," he said, gently placing slices of kimchi on his tongue, the wheel in his jaw winding around and around like a machine in peak performance.

He looked the same as he always did, but I caught a glimpse of myself in the corner of our video call. My eyes were little slits, swollen up by my fat, red cheeks and chin, my whole face looking like it was bee stung: *butthole eyes.* I hadn't spoken to anyone in a few days, or eaten, and had only heard my own voice when it took the form of a hot sob. I felt like I was dying, then felt furious that I wasn't. I would have to keep surviving when I clearly didn't want to—and more pressingly, when I clearly didn't know *how* to. I was crying again in front of my brother the way I had as a kid, unfiltered and without any sense of when it might stop. My brother has historically found me annoying, and I don't blame him, but I just never had his stony attitude toward life. I've aspired my whole life to remain as still as he's always been, and here he was, witnessing me at my most frenetic. My brother would handle a divorce with more grace. Or, rather, he wouldn't need one in the first place.

He would never speak first because he never speaks first. Even in this, he'd force me to start everything off. "Well," I said. "The good news is you're for sure Mom and Papa's favorite now."

He leaned back in his chair, throwing his head back and laughing, his big Adam's apple bobbing like bait. I did too, finally. It was funny because it was hell. It was funny because I couldn't die, and he wouldn't let me. He laughed the way he did about Lonnie Donegan, the way he laughs when something really delights and surprises him, and I felt proud to have made him laugh that way, even if it was because I was holding a match to my own life and hoping he could help me build a new one.

"Ahh," he said, winding his laugh down. "That's funny. That's funny!" He wiped a tear away, picked his chopsticks back up, and kept talking. I know he said other things that day. I know he helped me make a plan. I know he told me what to do with my money, and that I needed to find an apartment. I know he asked me if I was afraid, and I know I lied. All I really remember is the relief in still being able to make someone laugh, especially someone whose laugh felt like a prize.

◇

The timing of my mom's cancer made it crueler; she was diagnosed right as my divorce was finalized, a neat and nifty timeline for her paranoia. I only wanted a divorce; I didn't also order an existential crisis for my mother. "I don't understand," she said after the diagnosis became clear, when her surgery date was set, when we started reading brochures about what "we" could expect from radiation therapy. "I just had a knee replacement. I'm sick of being sick. How did this happen?" I didn't have an answer and nor did the doctors, who marveled at our extended family history featuring absolutely no cancer whatsoever.

When she started taking pain medication after her lumpectomy, my mother told me that her cancer was a direct result of my divorce. If you think I mean she *suggested* that, I don't mean that. What I mean is she said it: "I think this cancer is because of your divorce." She said it the way you might posit why your pie crust was coming out so dry. The drugs made her loopy and devastated, and she seemed to be having conversations in her head that I couldn't access. My mother had always been fiery and quickly frustrated, but she cooled down just as fast, and I was comfortable with the push/pull of her feelings. This was different. The drugs offered her anhedonia; she breezed through the hallways of the house like a Victorian ghost, wailing and beating her chest and asking what she did to merit cancer as a cosmic punishment.

Later, off the medication, she would have no memory of saying what she said, but it fit neatly in the canon of her pre-illness personality, even if it was cruel. She's superstitious in the way a lot of Indian mothers are, and I was raised with all her little worries. When I was young and would complain of a painful little bump on my tongue, she'd scold me for sins she'd already convicted me of. "Did you tell a lie?" she'd ask, her eyes narrowing as mine bulged. "You only get a bump on your tongue when you tell a lie. What lie did you tell?" I'd run through my seven-year-old memory for an example, which was easy to find: most people take to lying naturally.

I packed my things to head back home for a while—a month, maybe a few, whatever she needed. I no longer had a husband to run anything by, and I was unemployed for the first time in more than a decade. Two weeks before her biopsy results came in, I was laid off from a digital media company owned by an elder millennial in a zip-up American Apparel hoodie. The words "headline optimization training" and "do you want to join the DEIB committee, we only have two people and we need five" were already becoming relics of an unfamiliar past. I had all the time in the world, so long as my mother did. Which she would. My father and I were determined, dogged in her recovery, as if she even had a choice.

"We will make her whole," my father said when he first told me what her diagnosis was, like she was a Build-A-Bear with a torn stitch. He coughed out a clipped cry and handed the phone back to my mother. He wouldn't speak to me for another week or two, but I knew he wasn't ignoring me again.

He just couldn't look at me, with my mother's uneven hair-line and her curled upper lip and the dimple that forms through gnawing on the inside of our cheeks when we're nervous. I look like the person we're always on the brink of losing, a poor facsimile of what we want: my mother, eternal.

The cancer was in her breast, which she hated telling people. "Why do people ask where my cancer is?" she asked me over the phone a few weeks before her lumpectomy. "I told someone it was in my left breast the other day and do you know what she said to me? *That's so close to the heart.* Why would someone say that to me?"

I was furious for her, all this physical and emotional prob-ing she'd have to tolerate. "That person isn't a fucking doctor, Mom," I spat back. "Your heart isn't in your tit. They're not doing surgery on your heart." But woof, it felt like they were doing it on mine.

God. Saying that I experience my mother's pain is just so . . . *my mother* of me.

⚡

As soon as I became married, my parents softened on so many of my little rebellions and failures. New piercings were dismissed as none of their business. When I suggested that I might get a tattoo in the near future, my dad shrugged and then fell asleep with a speed not seen outside of coma patients. In the beginning of my marriage, sometimes I wouldn't be able to call because I was busy; it was the first time in my life that my mother accepted that as an excuse. "That's okay," she'd text back. "Spend some time with your husband." Later in my marriage when I couldn't call because I knew I would cry, I knew I would blurt out something I might regret, she remained the same. "That's okay," she'd text back. "Your husband will make you feel better." He never did, and I suspect she knew he wouldn't. She was just saying it to fill the air. It's just what you say when your daughter leaves your family to start a new one.

I can only speak for my little sliver of diaspora South Asians, but there's hardly a mechanism for getting divorced in our communities. No one talks about it. I'm the first divorce in my family, in all our generations of marriage records. There are plenty of reasons South Asian girls don't leave, from economic matters to child custody issues to plain fear. For a lot of us, we stay in our marriages because we don't know how to get back home.

"Aren't you lucky," I told my niece after my legal separation started. "I'm getting a divorce so it'll be a lot easier for you to do it later, if you want."

She nodded, then twelve and high off her own delicious, Gen Alpha fumes. "Thanks, Boo. I'll remember this when I'm thirty." Devastating. I wonder where she gets it from.

Indian weddings are about the girl, because they're sending her away. Boys get to stay home forever; their mothers move in and continue taking care of their child until their fingers curl and atrophy. But girls, untethered from home, are a risk. The hope is that she sails off somewhere better: to greater wealth, to a kind family. There's no belief she'll ever come back to her original home—her task is to build a new one.

There's no pressure to visit. You are to be subsumed by your husband.

But I never really left, not really. My parents never fully sent me away, and when I told them I had made a mistake—that word, "mistake," is tough to admit to an Indian parent—they brought me home. While I crashed at my friend's Park Slope apartment, no one related to me would leave me alone. (Trust me: I asked.) My cousin descended on me within a week, forcing me into the shower, into clothes, into a cab to look at apartments until I found one for myself. My brother's wife, a lawyer, helped me file for divorce, parsing through New York State's legalese to help me untangle myself from the mess I had drawn out far longer than I needed to. My parents brought me home. I became a Koul again, with little fanfare, and almost no guilt. (There had to be *some*. Look, they are who they are.) All my wedding gold was gifted to me by my side of the family; my mother told me to keep wearing it. "It's yours," she said. "It was only ever for you." I told her when I moved out that I still had the one piece of gold my ex-husband was given from our side of the family, a thin gold chain, from my bua to him years ago. He never wore it; yellow gold looked awful on his pink skin.

"So he doesn't have it?" she asked excitedly. When I confirmed, she pumped her fist. I still wear that necklace, too. It was only ever for me.

The only thing that kept me in my marriage for as long as it lasted was my mother; I didn't want to make her feel ashamed, even if I don't find anything inherently shameful about divorce.

"I was going to wait until you died," I told her when I visited, when I finally came home. "I thought I'd just wait for that, and then we could get a divorce. But it was taking you a long time."

"Next time, I'll try to go faster."

"That's nice of you to offer."

"I'm only staying alive to see you get remarried," she said, attempting to shift her tone to the serious while saying something absolutely fucking bonkers. "If it weren't for that, I could just lay down and die now."

"Good to hear, Mom," I said, adjusting her blankets and pillows and turning on the heating pad she had glued to where her stitches met. "You'll be alive a long time." I wonder how long it would have taken me to leave a bad marriage had I known coming home would be easier than I thought. There was always a way back.

"You know, ever since my first knee replacement, I walk a little slower," my mom told me. She has indeed slowed down, I can feel how it takes her a little longer to do everything. When I visit her, I'm only ever a few paces away. I follow her like I did as a kid, less for attention now and more in the way you hover around a delicate vase that's starting to wobble. "But whenever you walk with me," she said, "you always stop and turn around and look for me and wait. You wait for me when we walk." We had taken a stroll a few weeks earlier, her little sub-five-foot-tall body taking a bit longer to get down the sidewalk. That's okay. We weren't in a rush.

She ran her fingers along my hairline, getting grayer and grayer by the day. "I want that for you, too. I want someone to stop and look and wait for you." I've had trouble feeling a fulsome rage at my ex-husband for whatever he did to me, but I was always furious that he lied to my mother. Through me, he had made so many promises to her.

What I needed was to walk through a fire, not around it. My options felt limited at the time: I could circle the agni with a man who didn't love me, or I could walk through the flames and hope my mother would still be there. Everything would be painful, only for different reasons.

"Mom, *you* can stop and wait for me," I told her. "I don't need anyone else to do it."

"But I won't be here to do it forever." She's so dramatic; she's always right.

⚡

What we have struggled with is the inevitable. My mom knew a divorce was coming for me, long before I did; it's not like I would have listened to her even if she had warned me. I know she'll die; I can't look at that head-on, I can't bring myself to consider what it'll be like.

I've been rappelled back to my nuclear family, gladly. My father wrapped his head around my divorce quickly and easily. His main concern was whether or not I could capitalize on it, whether I'd ever be able to write the book that was sitting under contract for five years while I got married, realized it was a huge mistake, and got a divorce.

"As long as you're happy, nothing else matters," he said to me over the phone after I moved into my new apartment, sitting among the rubble of my life. "Well, actually, the only thing that matters is if you're creative. If a few books don't come out of this trauma, I don't know what the use of all this bloody trauma is. Trauma must generate something. I have a feeling it already has! Writers can't have nice things, everything like in a Bollywood cinema. No. It has to have some sort of turpitude, some sort of . . ."

He trailed off in his solo conversation, one of several he would have "with" me where I wouldn't even participate. He looked at my deadened eyes, my face sinking into itself. I knew I looked dead. "Good," he settled on. "I am happy to see you." He rushed off the phone, like he could cure my despair simply by never looking at it.

I couldn't redo my marriage or my divorce so I poured myself into my mother's care. I woke up with her and went to sleep with her rhythms. I looked at the bruise on her breast where they had removed the walnut-size tumor, the yellow and blue spreading across her skin like a wildfire. My skin would tingle at the same place where her stitches met. I plated her some crackers and cheese, which she would dutifully refuse to eat.

"Do you feel alone?" she asked me when she woke up. "I haven't been alone in so long. I don't know how I would do it."

"I've been alone a lot," I told her. "I was alone when I was married. I'm used to it." My mother knows that she knows very little about my marriage. She knows it wasn't good, but I don't like to bring her into the details of why or how, even when she asks. Our lives have always felt tethered, together and apart, and she's determined to feel what I feel, especially when it's painful or tragic. "I want to be sad *with* you," she told me, asking for more details, to know specifically what my husband said and how he said it and when he said it. Part of her, I suspect, wanted to figure out where I had gotten him wrong, and whether I could apologize and repair my marriage. A bigger part of her didn't understand what mal content looks like in a marriage. It was a feeling she'd never allowed herself.

But I was sad enough for the both of us, and I didn't want to share this part of it with her. What would it give her? Proof that I'd fucked up? There was no need.

It's more painful getting what you want and having it taken away, and for that truth only I wish I hadn't gotten married, to spare my mother the indignity of having it fall apart. I feel guilty about the money we spent. I feel bad about the time I wasted. My ex-husband and I did indeed fight so hard to have our relationship recognized by my family, to bring him into the fold. But what's the point of fighting, again? What am I doing so much of it for? I wish I hadn't begged my parents to reform their ideas around what my life could look like just for the result to be the same thing girls have been doing in my family since the late 1800s: a woman getting married to a man, hoping it would give her some-thing better.

In the weeks between her surgery and her treatments, I returned to New York and lit candles at the altars of the deities in my apartment. In my office are the small statues I had at my wedding—Parvati, Shiva, with their son Ganesh perched on their knees, a nuclear family. Nightly, I stood in front of them and begged for help with no surety that they could hear me. I'm not very religious, but maybe Parvati would listen if I cried loud enough. I would stand in flames for my mother. I would walk on hot coals to cure her. I worried they were tainted amulets I brought into my apartment from my cursed wedding, but I would take all the help I could get.

I'm not alone unless my mother leaves me alone.

But what happens to planets when they don't have a sun to orbit around?

⚡

How typical. How unbearably foreseen. To be a first-generation kid with a rebellious streak, eager to escape her parents' rules and culture, only to end up married to some white guy, who's wrong, wrong, wrong. How ridiculous to have to run back home. Only in hindsight does it seem obvious it would end up that way. My decisions always felt so final.

When my mother's oncologist met us with the results of her latest scans, I had by that point gotten used to tasting bile in my throat at all times. Months, almost years, had passed without her being in good health. When would another anvil fall on our heads? My entire life reshaped around her wellness. I was aware of every bite she ate, every minute she spent conscious. I could only build my life based on how healthy she was. I would have felt like this even with a husband, but without one, it was electric: What would I do without my mother?

After my wedding, when people asked me how it was, I always answered the same way: "My mom had a great time." Enduring is the image of her dancing in her stiff, light-green sari. She stopped dyeing her hair. She had eaten freely and had the only bite of cake I think anyone had at the reception, and so her body was strong and capable and lifted. There was joy there for her in my wedding, even if we each knew, separately, how doomed this was.

When she hugged me on my wedding day, she told me to be happy. I wept because I knew I wouldn't be. We both felt that this was not the place. There's a photo of the moment she hugged me at the mandap, and it's the only photo from that week I still love. I'm crying into her shoulder harder than I knew I had the capacity for. It looks like a picture of two halves refusing to split. I sobbed because I knew I would have to tell her the truth, eventually: I spent so long being so unhappy, despite the promise I made. I wouldn't be able to outrun how miserable I was. I'd have to make her miserable with my news, too.

And so, when the doctor told her she was cancer-free, that her treatments had worked, that it had not spread, I cried again. I collapsed into my own hands, relieved and grateful for this good news, finally. She laughed and smiled, perched on the examination table in size five wedge sandals, looking as usual like she somehow knew what was coming before it did. She looked like she was in on the good news. We had staved off death, for a little while. We had rebuilt my life, for now, and would soon rebuild hers, too. We had fought so hard, and could maybe now let down our guards. My dad and I orbited around my mom once more, happily. We'll have to figure something else out one day, but not today.

On my wedding day, my mother asked me to be happy. Years later, divorced and unemployed and embittered and anointed by flame at last, I'd be able to answer her for good. While her posture got a little straighter, a little more hopeful, I could finally reassure her that I was not untethered in the world, not really, at least not quite yet. I emerged on fire, with the truth: *I'm happy, Mom. This time, I mean it. I'm happy.*

KALI STARTS
A FIRE

⚡

What was I supposed to do? Sit around and eat fruit?

I can remember my ex-husband's kindnesses when I see other people experience similar versions of them. I meet a couple at Janet's engagement party, and they tell me the same story together, each of them speaking a few lines before the other takes over. They operate as one, and I remember when I used to feel synced to someone else's heartbeat. Two women on a date eat off each other's plates at Raoul's in SoHo; that shorthand was one of the few things I loved about our kind of monogamy. Teenagers kiss in the park, as if the world has already ended.

But why do I try to remember when he was kind? It doesn't comfort me. It only reminds me that once, I had fooled myself into thinking my devotion would be recompensed. It's helpful, sometimes, to remind myself of all the ways he made me miserable. It gives me resolve. I was right to run.

When Parvati is too soft, and when even Durga isn't fierce enough, Parvati's final form is beckoned. Kali is an oft-feared Hindu goddess, a destructive but essential female god in Hinduism. You've probably seen her before, her eyes wide and spooky, tongue hanging out, a garland of skulls around her neck, blood on her hatchet and hands, thick breasts and thighs, and a shield of black hair. She's usually depicted trampling on Shiva, her blue body victorious but serene.

Some Hindus don't like speaking to or about Kali, even if we all know she's necessary to the pantheon. My aunties don't like speaking her name, offering her silent reverence. Kali emerges from Durga, the darkest form of the most maternal deity. She's a divine protector, a force of time. She is inevitable, setting the universe ablaze so that we can start over. Hindus believe in reincarnation and in the potential for starting fresh; through Kali, we can achieve "moksha," meaning eternal release and liberation from the cycle of reincarnation. Kali teaches us our fucking lesson.

The night after our wedding, I looked at my Parvati statue while my new husband snored next to me. I didn't know what I didn't know about my marriage—that my husband was having an affair, that he was about to shrink my world down to his needs and his desires and his fits of fury—but already I felt uneasy in the way we tethered ourselves to each other. Did part of me like my husband because he represented a surefire fight? Yes: it was where I felt safest, it was a role I inhabited easily. But once the fight was over, once we were a couple and my father was finally able to say his name without wincing, there was no fight to be had. Who was I without this central conflict? If he and I weren't united against an external force, then what were we? Did that make us adversaries? Had I turned him into one because I didn't know what else to do with myself? Is my brain that primitive, that if I don't see prey nearby, I'll eat one of my own?

I couldn't tell if Parvati was standing in protest to show her devotion, or to have her wishes be taken seriously. As a child, I had to be loud to be noticed. Throughout my life, "no" could be ignored, but "NO" would be respected. Parvati's parents didn't want her to marry Shiva, and the texts say she meditated in fire to prove to them that she was devoted to him. I don't like this reading, and I want to be able to reject it for that reason alone. If marriage was her only way through life, could it be that her protestations were for herself, and not for her husband? She tortured herself and everyone around her until they saw her autonomy. *She* would pick. She would make her own destiny.

Kali comes to battle Raktabīja, an *asura*, or antigod. Raktabīja was particularly strong thanks to his own boon: just as Parvati had received a boon to marry Shiva, Raktabīja was granted one that allowed his power to increase every time a drop of his blood was spilled. He multiplied on the battlefield in the thousands. No god could stop him, though Durga tried. With every attempted strike, the blood he shed turned into additional members of his army. They laughed in her face as she struggled to destroy the evil infiltrating the grounds.

Durga is kind until mocked. Enraged by being belittled, Durga transmuted into Kali and filled the sky with her shrieking cackle. She consumed Raktabīja and his army, drank his blood, set fire to the earth he tried to inherit, and danced in victory.

Kali is depicted as standing on Shiva's body, because that's the only way the gods could get her to snap out of her rampage. Nothing could stop her once she started, and if she continued to rage, soon she'd consume the entire universe. Shiva called out to her, and she heard nothing but the sound of her own laughter. And so, to stop her destruction, he threw himself at her feet. It was a show of desperation, but a show of love: Parvati showed her dedication, and so Shiva did too when she needed it most.

For me, it was too late. My ex-husband tried to keep me in the same way, throwing himself at my feet in a show of belated devotion. He begged me to stop, to cease my destruction. *You're going to end our world. You're leaving us bloodless. We won't survive this.*

I didn't care. I had been Parvati for so long. I wouldn't regress, no matter how much he cried.

My mother's mother, Durga, was married by the time she was fourteen years old. My own mother was married by twenty-four. By thirty-four, I have fought for the hard-won privilege of possibly choking on a kebab in my apartment and dying alone. I'm grateful. I've earned this.

⚡

My childhood neighbor Lana moved out one day, and I lost touch with her. Her brother was gone soon after that. My parents said they heard Lana's parents arguing more. They divorced, an ugly, contested split that ended years after it started. This was the family that I thought represented the most even-tempered and wholesome type of North American community. My family came from the bog and Lana's lived in the light. Sometimes it feels like there is so little I can remember about my marriage and my divorce and the thousand little cuts that I endured, and other times, I remember so much, so vividly, that it feels like I might still be living in someone else's life.

"He's too old to cheat on me," I said to people who came to meet me on my first book tour. I made this joke blithely when people asked if I had advice on how to find—and keep—a husband. People thought I held some key to this, and maybe for a while I thought I did too. When was the last time I said this? I was in Edmonton, or maybe Halifax, or possibly Wisconsin, or was it San Francisco? So much of my first book charted our course to a wedding, and so people were happy to see my left hand hung heavier. "Strongly recommend being engaged to an old man," I told a woman in line for a signed book. "They're just more settled. You don't have to deal with watching them struggle to grow up."

A week before our first wedding anniversary, I had found

out about his long-standing affair. For the entirety of our marriage, I couldn't find him. I couldn't reach him, wherever he was. Maybe his mind was with the woman he was lying to me about, or maybe it was with someone else entirely, but I suspect he had himself locked away for the most part. I always thought marriage meant the exact opposite. I thought that was the whole point.

Throughout our relationship, the fighting proved comforting to me. If we were arguing, that meant there was something left to argue for. Fighting was a joint mission; the goal was to save each other. The logic, in hindsight, doesn't make a lot of sense, as if I thought strangling each other was the way to give us more oxygen. But it was the only way I had learned to move through life. I had never gotten anything without a fight first, and now, we'd have a fight second, too. My parents fought, but they loved each other. I was missing half of the equation.

I didn't know what to do after finding out about his affair other than to take us to couples therapy immediately. Our therapists, of which we had several, all brittle little white women who looked like their names were Teresa, lauded us for trying so hard to make it work. "There had to have been something huge to keep you two together for so long, and against such odds," Teresa 3 said to us. At the time, I liked hearing it; it made me feel like the work was worth it, like there was something cosmic there. Now, it sounds like boring platitudes from a woman paid to try to heal what was built broken. I wanted our therapists to give me permission to quit, but I knew none of them would. How would we continue our out-of-pocket payments if Teresas 1 through 6 told us what was becoming abundantly clear to me: we were not destined to stay together.

In Hudson, he walked a half-step behind me all weekend, deferential and afraid that I would leave him. My parents had just hit their fortieth wedding anniversary. We faltered in year one, and thinking about it made me soak every inch of sidewalk in town with my loud, unrelenting tears. I was so desperate to reach out and touch him but I knew he didn't deserve it. I hated myself for my own sympathies toward him. I hated it when he cried. "Tell me how to fix it," he pleaded with me, but I didn't have an answer. I had never been violated in this particular way. I had never had my own optimism in someone else thrown back in my face like this.

"Do you still love me?" my husband asked me when I found out about his affair. When he wept at my silence, I finally stopped feeling like I was standing on hot coals. Finally, a fire of protection. I built it myself.

⚡

A good fight has an end. It needs to, otherwise you're just in a trap of your own design. I'd rather fight with someone I love than with a stranger. I'm more inclined to start a fight with a friend than with a rude bartender. There's catharsis in fighting with someone you love; if you're lucky, you get a resolution to your problem and a makeup, or at minimum, you get it out of your system. In the home where my brother and I grew up, our parents would fight and then the fight would settle. But my ex-husband's parents were divorced, as we would soon be. He understood how a divorce could change you; he remembered all fights, ours and theirs too, while I could barely recall if we'd had one that day. He didn't have the ease I did, that I could tell him I hoped he died and then an hour later ask what's for dinner.

I thought Lana was weak for not being able to fight. I thought that because she didn't have an appetite for conflict she didn't know how to muscle through an unfair world. But I had chosen a fight, and picked a fellow fighter to marry— that dynamic was comfortable and familiar. I watched my parents fight and thought that was a pattern to repeat, but my parents each made the active choice to live in conflict for-ever. I didn't have to do that. I could outgrow it. Fighting and fury isn't the only path to love; it was just the one I knew best.

There were years, between finding out about my hus-band's affair and our eventual divorce, when I wanted to pretend it hadn't happened. I spent a few days trying to decide if I was the type of person who could deny my own feelings. But the more time passed, the more our fights lingered with me and began to shift. Old memories of still-bubbling conflicts started to come back to me; I had a mental dossier of everything he did that ever bothered me, and a catalog of my own related failures, too. I could easily access a memory about how he slapped my phone out of my hand in an Uber after a party (I got a one-star rating after that ride), or when he said my new glasses made me look like Groucho Marx (true, but unnecessary to verbalize), or when I did a pirouette in front of him before heading out to my company's Christmas party and he looked at my sequin pants and asked me why I didn't take the garbage out that afternoon. I remembered my own failings, too, don't worry: I remembered how I got too drunk at one of his work events and screamed at him in front of his colleagues, or when I told him I couldn't wait to get away from him once the quarantine ended, or when I sneered at him, "You're just like your father, and you're just like mine, too."

I used to like it when he fought with me because it meant he loved me. I could once close my eyes, and imagine that kisses and cruelties were the same thing, that the sting of love and loathing offered the same kind of intimacy. My ex-husband used to laugh about a *Key & Peele* sketch, where a young couple argues until the woman storms off. Instead of letting her walk away, her boyfriend follows her, screaming, "Meegan, you forgot your jacket!" She does not turn around; she's only in it for the passion of an argument. My ex thought this was a perfect diagram of our relationship: "See? It's me trying to help you and you running off and starting a fight." He laughed; I thought about whether he and Cait would have laughed at me when he ripped the condom wrapper open. I once asked him if it was blue; he looked at me like I had spoken in tongues.

Our fights sank into our skin like tattoos; we emerged pockmarked and transformed. Once, I could regenerate a limb blown off by a verbal attack, and I could do it in minutes. Now, in the aftermath of our split, I see how much longer my recovery time is. I'm sadder. I'm not so petty anymore. I've lost the zeal for conflict, but as our relationship was starting to wind down, I wasn't fully equipped to release him from the fight. No peace for my husband. No release from this humiliation he bestowed upon me. I was unfair. It's my only regret.

What I wanted was space—sometimes literally. I wanted it to be possible for me to carefully and thoughtfully build a rocket for one, outfitted with the most powerful engine known to humanity, big enough just for my body and a paperback or two, a few packs of Dramamine, and maybe my good pair of glasses. I would slip into the rocket, seal myself inside, and shoot myself directly into the sun, with one of two possible outcomes: either I would die instantly, burned alive before I even made contact, my skin and bones melting away and my entire corporeal form vanished and forgotten for good, *or* I would somehow survive it, and become one with the most fiery substance in the universe. In either case, wouldn't that be fitting? Just two roiling, gaseous hotheads colliding and bursting in a multiverse explosion. I wanted to be alone because I didn't want to fight, but fighting was all I've ever been good at, and fighting was ill-advised during a once-in-a-lifetime (*one hopes*) pandemic.

The way I used to roll "husband" around in my mouth like a minty candy, I started floating words like "first husband" or "ex-husband" or "estranged husband." I went from Rich Salad Mom to Mysterious Divorcée in my own head, swanning around in floral robes, a martini in hand, a glint in my eye that said, *He didn't go missing, I just killed him.* But I didn't like "ex-husband" that much either; it felt so hostile, which wasn't really how I felt about him. I missed him even when he stood in front of me, stirring wine into the paella pan. I missed him even when he held my hand in the way he did, just my pinky and ring fingers wrapped around his. I missed him even when I knew I had to leave for good, that missing him would be a permanent affliction.

I sold a story, to you and to myself, about my marriage. I renamed him in text, calling him *Hamhock* in my first book. There's no plausible nickname for him here. You can't call your ex a cutesy nickname in print, but a pseudonym doesn't work quite right either. Anything feels like a transgression, and there's no point in giving a ghost a name anyway. Strangers from the internet flooded my inbox with congratulations when I got married. I wrote a love story without even realizing it, and then felt trapped by the conclusion I knew everyone wanted. So I gave an audience of my friends and family and, yes, some strangers a good ending to a universal story: we fought for love, and we won, against all odds. The story I wrote was true, for a while: that we were perfect for each other, our match was cosmic, I didn't need Vedic astrology to tell me I had made a good choice.

Some of my stories are dishonest, even if they were true at the time. But we all need the stories we tell ourselves; it's good to romanticize some of your own experiences in order to stay alive. The story I told myself was, first, that I had to fight to survive, that it was my only way to exist in the world, and second, that any fight that came to my door was a fight worth the exhaustion. I skinned my knuckles and broke my fingers and wore myself out, flailing my arms wildly with no strategy. I just wanted to be wrong about what I knew was going to happen regardless.

Years later, I'd ask Cait about her affair with my husband. Was it worth it? Did they think about me at all? Did she try to stop seeing him? Did he try to stop? Why tell me, after years of keeping it a good, tight secret? I never suspected a thing, which only made me feel even more foolish than I already did. She has some answers, not all.

"People warned me about him when I first met him. I just didn't listen. I didn't want to hear it. He was so fucking awful to me and I just kept going back," she told me. "I thought it was cool that this older, mature guy liked me." Cait has a slight smile and sad eyes and, yes, narrow, white hips. None of that protected her, even if in my imagination I thought it did. "It makes me really, really sad to think about that version of myself."

"Did you think I was stupid?" I asked her. She admitted that neither she nor my ex-husband considered the optics: two white people, both older than me, sharing this ugly secret behind my back while I wrote about my new life as a wife. "Were you two just laughing at me, at how little I knew?"

"Absolutely not," she said. "He preyed on you, too,

Scaachi." In three conversations, she apologized eight times more than my ex-husband did in almost four years of marriage. I know, because I counted.

I thought Cait had built an understanding of my doomed marriage from the internet trail I left behind; it turns out she was just young and misguided and hopeful. Cait was trying to find purpose in the fight, too. It wasn't about me; I was just the body between her and the place where she had fixed her hopes.

When I started telling my friends that I was looking for my own apartment, I was always met with their weepy Margaret Keane eyes and the same refrain: "I know how hard you fought." I never fully knew what they meant. Were they saying they knew how hard I fought to keep us together? To make things feel like they once did when I was twenty-two and everything he did made me feel an excited buzz in my stomach? Did they understand the incredible labor and time and blood and tears, so many tears, we put into our union, making its failure that much more undignified? Or, were they saying that they knew how much *we* fought? Did they recognize how caustic we could be, how we'd lock horns and grow intent on embarrassing each other in public?

It's so humiliating, sometimes, to be seen.

When we separated our books, we fought about that, too. I wanted to keep my original David Sedaris books, my high school copy of *The Catcher in the Rye*, books we'd had duplicates of when we moved in together, his going into donation.

We went through every book, crying and yelling and waiting for someone to pop out of the first edition of *A Heartbreaking Work of Staggering Genius* that he bought me for our anniversary and tell us this was all a sick joke, that we were fine, we didn't have to do this. But if we were still fighting about books, I knew we'd find other fights if we stayed together, if we tried one last time to make it work. We loved each other and I always thought that any refusal to fight was tantamount to defeat. But when he said he wanted to keep the Lahiris, books on critical race theory (he probably needed them more than me), and novels written by our friends and signed to both of us, I did the unthinkable: I didn't put up a fight. He could have them. I could always buy more books. Walking away from a fight isn't cowardice; sometimes it's the only way to win.

He kept *Lolita*. I kept *Heartburn*. See? Another lousy metaphor.

$\frac{}{}$

I think I'm more of a Kali than a Parvati these days. Parvati is known for her dedication, her purity, and her self-sacrifice, usually for the men in her life: her husband, her community, her children, and finally the gods she comes to defend as Durga. But Kali's stated purpose is to destroy evil, even if that means being a doomsday teller. When Durga needs more fight, she transforms into Kali, who ultimately has the courage to do what others won't. She'll kill things. She'll start over. She's known as the Dark Mother: to give birth to anything, something else has to end. She is wrath embodied. I needed her so much.

The night before my thirty-first birthday was the last conversation I had with my husband when I still called him my husband. It had been three years since I learned of his affair, which he promised was his first and last. The pandemic hit us just a few months after I found out, forcing us to stay together, literally stuck in our limited square footage. But the world had now reopened. Time had passed, and yet, I felt the same. We fought in a new way that night. It felt like we were crossing a Rubicon that we'd never return from, like this fight would indeed be worse than all the others. He looked at me with a shark-like emptiness, like I was chum. We had stopped fighting for each other and instead viewed one another as the enemy. This kind of argument was rendering our marriage unsalvageable with every word we shared. No one knows us better than our enemies or our spouses; to have one person inhabit both roles is to be tortured in your own home.

"You cause all of this shit," he told me, which was tough to take seriously because he was wearing his finest cotton jam-jams. "You cause all these problems. We fight because of you and only you." I considered his argument: That the full universe of trouble we had as a couple was entirely because of me. Just me. Me, who could not figure out our gas bill, who had the lower credit score, who was too young to know better until I was too old to make better decisions. Incompetent, unimportant, inconsiderate me. I had done all this? Who knew I had such power, and over a white man with a platinum card, the kind that clattered when you dropped it.

Parvati's story only exists in the context of her husband. She is an icon of duty. She will make things right. If Shiva asked her to exile herself for him, she would. In the stories my mother told me about her, Shiva never directed her to do anything. She did it herself. She knew her place before she was asked.

My husband didn't know how sick I was of losing grip of all these stories—ones I told myself about my mother, about God, about him and our doomed union. He didn't know how exhausted I was by having to take into account his version of events. At some point during the marriage, thoughts about myself and my own life were replaced with thoughts about him and his exigencies. The only safe place I had anymore were among my own thoughts; I mostly kept them to myself.

Or, I wrote them down, as I have done since I was a child. Throughout my life, and through our marriage, I kept up with rigorous journaling and note-taking, recording whatever came to mind mostly so it could exit my brain as soon as possible. My journals used to be full of anecdotes about crushes and internships; then it was about falling in love and pleading with my parents to believe that it was a real love. The last night we spoke to each other, I knew my journal was full of uncharitable thoughts about my marriage. I didn't know I wanted to leave, but I knew I didn't want to stick around.

"You're going to do this on your birthday?" my husband said to me as we argued on the cusp of my thirty-first, as if it was a crime against him to ruin my own birthday. "I planned all these nice things for you, but you're going to ruin it."

I wrapped my arms around myself and thought about the way my dad would sing to me: *It's my paaaaarty, I'll cry if I waaaaant to.* My father, flawed and impossible and argumentative, always let me cry. When he told me my mother had cancer, I burst into tears on the phone with him while I was at work, and he made room for it. "It's okay," my dad had told me, his voice small but sturdy. "You can cry. That's allowed. You can always cry to me."

My husband laughed mirthlessly when my tears started. "Do you want a divorce?" he asked me. It didn't feel like a question, but instead like a challenge.

"I don't know," I told him, which was a lie. I did.

"Well, let's find out." He marched into our bedroom with a clear mission, and returned holding a lime-green notebook aloft, his face red and my heart pounding so hard I needed him to repeat twice what he said to me next: "Yes, I read your journal."

He didn't like what he read: my true feelings about our marriage, my quest to be loved still unfulfilled, my itch to be witnessed by someone and not merely visualized. He had never been so angry with me before, and his rage outpaced even mine after I had found out about his affair years earlier. I had not fully forgiven him, but I had learned to walk in lockstep with him again, pretending we were on the same team. But he had trespassed against me again, this time by spinning the top of my skull open, peering into my brain, and then criticizing me for its contents. Even the puerile nature of his intrusion seemed designed to make me feel immature. That I left him because he read my diary was so juvenile compared with what else we had confronted.

"Should I read from it?" he asked, humiliating me and humiliating me and humiliating me. I flung myself at his feet to try to stop his rage; I ran to our bathroom, the only door in our apartment that locked. He compared our failures of each other as tantamount to the same thing; his affair was identical to my thought crimes. "You think you're better than me?" he asked. "You're not."

"My thoughts aren't safe in this house!" I screamed from the other side of the bathroom door, unhinged, unraveled, enraged. "You won't even let me be safe in my own mind." He mocked me for being maudlin with my words. I had heard this criticism from him before, and in the past it only pulled me closer to him. Only he could insult me, and so only he could soothe the burn.

He kicked at the door and turned the knob uselessly. "Fucking unlock the door," he said. "I'm going to fucking bust the door. You want me to fucking do it? You know I will."

Kali can bloom for herself. If her husband is the cause of her flames, she doesn't need to stop her well-earned destruction just to spare his ego. She knows when something has to end.

I left him on the morning of my thirty-first birthday. My mother called to marvel at how long she and I had been alive together.

For years, I wrote in my journals thinking I was telling my story on my own terms. In my work, my husband was always standing over my shoulder, monitoring the narrative, passively suggesting I tell it a certain way. The only thing I held on to throughout my marriage was the story I was telling myself about it; but the only place I was honest about our marriage's true state was in that lime-green notebook. He took both away, first with his affair, and later, by violating the only privacy and safety I had left.

I'm forgetting what my ex-husband looked like. I'm forgetting how sharp the tip of his nose was, how his blond brows would knit together, the rough terrain of his fingernails when he chewed them during a football game. I'm forgetting the ways he hurt me, but I'm also forgetting what kept me with him for so long. I don't miss him, but I instead miss something more potent: I miss the surety I had when I was with him. I was *so* sure. I was so confident. I could not fail so long as I was one part of a two-piece unit. I thought I knew who he was, but more than that, I thought I knew who I was. I was wrong about both, and letting the truth unfurl in front of me is a task I didn't anticipate when I slid a ring on his finger and promised him seven steps around the agni. Sometimes it felt good to live in the wrong. Sometimes I wish I could go back to that; take the blue pill and sink back into sleep.

In the wake of forgetting, I remember something better. I did not need to stay the same person I was at twenty. Something can be doomed and still happening right on schedule. I no longer dream of ceasing my own needs—I don't hope to shrink down so small that my husband doesn't see me, nor do I hope to stay alone forever, biding my time in solitude. In the wake of forgetting, I remember myself and how I exist. I was tasked with taking care of myself from birth, and for a while I left me to the wolves. For so much of my life I've stood on the outside looking in, watching how shabbily I've treated me for so long. *Why am I doing this to her?* I wrote in my journal one afternoon, hollowed out from fighting for something I didn't even want anymore. *I thought I loved her.*

⚡

I take an exercise class in Tribeca periodically, a sixty-minute cardiac arrest masquerading as fitness. I'm not sure if the class improves my heart health or if it's toning any part of me, but I don't go because of the physical benefits. I like going because the gym seems to host a kind of First Wives Club of lower Manhattan. Every class is full, every mat hosting a woman who either is a first wife or is en route to being a first wife. Everyone is wealthy, some moderately famous, the details about their divorces previously written about in *Page Six* or maybe DeuxMoi. Some of them wear a full face of makeup, big hoop earrings, hair wraps and false eye-lashes, more Van Cleef jewelry than I think the building is insured to carry. I attend this class with the same curiosity and reverence I might bring to the zoo. *Oh, look at her*, I think to myself when one of the regulars comes to class wearing an engagement ring the size of my ass. *A fresh one.*

I can tell that our divorces are different but I feel a kinship with these wild animals. We're all so brittle. Everyone seems like they're used to a cage and this is the only time they get out in the yard, to stretch their arms and chests. The class starts when the music swells and the animals are usually cry-ing within the first five minutes. We hop and flop and sob and leap and dive and wiggle around, like we're having reli-gious experiences. The women roar out their days, they pant and yelp and whoop and weep and wail; their feelings are huge and so close to the surface, it feels like they've been holding everything in until they were free to scream in this candlelit studio. It is exhausting.

The teachers are too friendly, too warm—at the end of the first class I took, one of them made a beeline to me after class and said, forcefully: "I would like a hug." I let her crunch her bony body against the pools of sweat on my chest. I leave every class with my legs vibrating, like I could levitate. The more I go, the closer I get to crying in public. It hasn't hap-pened yet; there's still some emotional membrane I can't quite break through in the wild. But here are all these ani-mals, growling and mewling and breaking down and building back up among each other. Do they know what we all have in common? I wonder if they've been as sad as I've been. I wonder if they feel as free as I do.

I suspect my ex feels like one day I floated off into space and never returned. Over the course of our marriage, I got stronger and more strident and let myself drift away from him and into my own hands. In my divorce, I returned to my own possession. The only hard part of leaving him, ultimately, was realizing how much I had abandoned myself. Fighting meant family, comfort, intimacy—I only fought with the people I loved and who loved me most. I had never been abandoned by any of the people I fought with, no matter how loud our arguments got. I'm sure Lana's family heard them, from time to time. But our family stuck together.

And yet, the fight I was having in my marriage required me to forget myself. I had to pick a side, for the first time in my life—we were not fighting on the same team. For the first time, it was between possessing myself or possessing nothing. What other choice could I make? On the other side of divorce, I'd meet myself again and I was hopeful to be forgiven for how long I abandoned her there. I entered this room to eventually learn how to leave it.

I packed my things and moved out in record time. Baby Braga flew in from Toronto to help me, a radio signal from ground control asking, "I know you said you're okay, but *are* you okay?" We drove to a suburban New Jersey Target and I bought a rug. Braga put up $800 worth of press-and-stick wallpaper, turning my home into a millennial Pinterest playground. We called my Wi-Fi network "The Pussy Palace" and my Bluetooth television "Vulva Vision." When I bought a mirror with pom-poms on it, he looked at me with slight alarm. "I don't think I knew your tastes were so . . . vivid." He took me to Margaritaville for my birthday, a sweet but ill-fated attempt to cheer me up. My body wouldn't let me be drunk, but his would, and he drank so many doubles that slugs of vomit poured out of him while hanging out of a cab in the East Village.

Janet saged my apartment and brought a framed photograph of herself. Barb texted every fifteen minutes. Kiara sent flowers. Adrian sent wine. On my bookshelf I placed my Shiva and Parvati statuettes from my wedding, the same ones that once stood in auspicious honor at our head table. My mother called two, three, sometimes five times a day. "You don't know how hard this is on me," she'd say without a single iota of traceable irony.

My friends left, the flowers died, I drank all the wine. Nothing survives me, but nothing is designed to. Everyone is just a visitor here, even me. Still, I welcome the tourists.

⚡

A year after our breakup, I was unsure of how to celebrate the anniversary of my proverbial freedom. A year had not been enough time for me to know how I felt about my new life—by that point, I had yet to be laid off, and my mother had yet to be diagnosed with cancer. Still, I woke up every day with a lump of uncertainty in my throat. And so my friends and I decided it was best not to wallow in New York; *What the hell*, we said, *let's go on a quick vacation.*

Nine of us went to Miami, the scene of a few crimes. When I was engaged, my friends and I came to Miami to celebrate my bachelorette. A few years later, I'd take the same trip with my husband, the beginning of the end of our relationship.

The trip was not intended to be an emotional bloodletting. All we wanted to do was go to Mac's Club Deuce, a dive bar that's been open since the 1920s and still somehow allows smoking inside. My only ask was that I make no decisions, and so dinner reservations, evening excursions, and beach days were all planned by someone else; I was only told where to go. And since I asked for no details, it surprised me along with everyone else that the hotel we were staying at was the same one my ex-husband and I stayed in, years earlier, when our marriage was first starting to spoil.

"We can just get another hotel," Braga said, but I only half heard him. I was too busy laughing.

My friends and I retreaded the same trip I'd had with my ex-husband, mostly by accident: We played darts and smoked Belmonts and drank beers like water was illegal. We went to the hookah bar and walked along the beach. We ate perhaps a million stone crabs, washed down with herbaceous cocktails that cost $28.

"One martini is good," Adrian slurred, spilling his drink in my lap, "but have you ever had THREE martinis?"

Janet had, which she announced thusly while pulling an olive off its spear: "ADRIAN, I'VE HAD MORE MARTINIS TONIGHT THAN YOU'VE HAD IN YOUR ENTIRE LIFE."

It had been a full year, which should have felt monumental, but instead it felt like nothing. Plenty of my life was different, but so much of it was the exact same.

On our last day in Miami, sunburned (Braga) and hungover (Braga and Adrian) and dreading reality (me), we decided I needed something ceremonial to close out my trip. I'd brought with me one piece of ephemera that the boys had given me on my bachelorette party in Miami years prior: a pink sash with glittering gold letters printed on, custom-made for the silly little party they threw for me, ostensibly because I was making this enormous, irreversible decision. It feels so frivolous now; we were acting so grown-up.

"Let's take it to the ocean," Adrian said. "Hurl it into the sea! Speak in tongues to the water gods! Let the sharks take it!"

But when we got to the edge of the tide, our Canadian sensibilities took over. "Isn't this . . . *littering*?" Braga asked. He said the word "littering" like it was child abuse.

"Maybe don't throw it into the water. Just, drown it for a little while," Adrian said.

I took a few steps into the water, kids playing on the beach and frat boys falling asleep in the sand, and held the sash underwater. It unfurled in my hands, the sparkle of the text gleaming in the sun. "Future Ms. Hamhock," it said. I held it underwater, strangling a bad memory.

A small crowd of people started to applaud. Hunched over the sash, this idol of a successful failure, I thought for a moment I was being praised for this palimpsest of sorts.

Look at me! I'm reclaiming my life! The ocean is a metaphor because, when you get divorced, everything is!!!

But alas, it wasn't about me, because nothing is ever that personal. A few feet from me, a couple was getting engaged in the sand. On one knee, he placed a ring on her finger, and they promised each other the covenant I was unbinding: forever, forever, forever. We clapped for her alongside everyone else. I'm okay, periodically, with being wrong.

I balled the sash up into a wet pile, and walked back to the street, tossing it in the trash—no need to make more of a mess. Behind us, the newly engaged couple was hanging off each other, resplendent in the joy of potential. She got on the phone to call her mom. He watched her gawk at her ring, a totem of their hopes yoked together.

I took off my sunglasses and closed my eyes, turning my face toward the sun; I'm still getting used to standing in the light. It's just so freakish to want to love someone else, isn't it? What a stupid thing to do. What an unbelievable waste of my time. What a way to make me hurt and hurt and hurt and hurt. I wonder when I'll get to try it again.

MOKSHA

RELEASE FROM
SAṂSĀRA

"I will hunch my shoulders and wait,
Claws sharpened,
Teeth agape."

—TANYA TAGAQ, "TEETH AGAPE"

A COMPREHENSIVE LIST OF EVERYTHING MY DAD HAS CALLED BERGDORF GOODMAN

⚡

Bergman Bergdorf
Bergman Goodman
Bergeldorfman's
Bergdorf Hoffman
Bergdoor Hoffman
Bergdoor Johnson
Bergman's Bergman
Goodman Goldstein
Bubblegum
Double Man
Duffer Band
Guggenheim & Woodwork
The Boogenheim
The Googleheim
Häagen-Dazs
Bügle Dusseldorf
Guggenheim Shop
Bergfordman Bodega-Goodman's

ACKNOWLEDGMENTS

My endless gratitude to the people who made this book—and my career—possible: to Ron Eckel at CookeMcDermid Literary Management; Anna deVries, Laura Clark, and the team at St. Martin's Press; Martha Kanya-Forstner, Kristin Cochrane, Ashley Dunn, and Emma Ingram at Knopf Canada.

My friends became inadvertent first-draft readers, and so I'm indebted to them for listening to my feelings in their ugliest forms: Elamin Abdelmahmoud, Rosalind Adams, Jenna Amatulli, Matthew Braga, Angelina Chapin, Adrian Cheung, Molly Coldwell, Haley Cullingham, Anne Donahue, Supriya Dwivedi, Emmanuel Dzotsi, Lakna Edirisinghe, Kelly Farber, Isaac Fitzgerald, Michael Goldlist, Danielle Henderson, Jamilah King, Rudy Lee, Jane Lytvynenko, Vicky Mochama, Caroline Moss, Miranda Newman, Albert Samaha, Barbora Simkova, Sarah Thyre, and Karolina Waclawiak.

My parents gave me this life and returned me to it over and over. I'll spend my current existence and the next trying to make something they're proud of. My gratitude to my brother and his family, and my cousins Angela Misri and Anita Dhar, for craning me up and out.

But thank you, above all, to Kiara Kent, my editor at Knopf Canada, my North Star, the strongest tether I have to hope. My work has always been in your hands, but my spirit has been, too. This book wouldn't exist today without you, but then again, neither would I.

ABOUT THE AUTHOR

Barbora Simkova, Simkova Studios

Scaachi Koul is a senior writer for *Slate* and a cohost of the Ambie Award–winning podcast *Scamfluencers*. She cohosted the Emmy-nominated Netflix series *Follow This*, and her writing has appeared on *This American Life* and in *The New Yorker, New York*, and *The Cut*. You can also find her in documentaries, including *Quiet On Set* and *Pretty Baby*. Her bestselling book, *One Day We'll All Be Dead and None of This Will Matter*, was a *New York Times* Editors' Choice. You can follow her on Instagram and on her Substack, *Hater Nation*. She lives in Brooklyn.